Me!?

A Curriculum for Teaching Self-Esteem Through an Interest Center

JO ELLEN HARTLINE

Illustrated by
MELODY HARTLINE-BUCKNER

Paid for from:
AOD Program Funds
Eau Claire Area School District
500 Main Street
Eau Claire, WI 54701

Zephyr Press
Tucson, Arizona

Copyright © 1982 by Jo Ellen Hartline
Revised Edition © 1990 by Zephyr Press

Library of Congress Number 82-90750

ISBN: 913705-43-8

CONTENTS

FOREWORD

The greatest treasure in a school is the student. Perhaps a coequal "greatest treasure" might be a creative and caring teacher. Jo Ellen Hartline's plea that all of us become that coequal treasure and the practical suggestions for helping us along the road deserve reading and rereading. Children learn to love only from being loved and our access to teaching them comes from their belief that we do love them. This book points the way.

Edward E. Ford, coauthor
For the Love of Children
and *Permanent Love*

PREFACE

My journey as a teacher has been an exciting and rewarding one. When I started teaching in the late 1950s, I never dreamed that my work would lead me into an intensive study of self-esteem. It began with my own need. I once read that we teach that which we most need to learn. This has been my case. When my husband died very suddenly at the age of 34, I felt totally unprepared to face life alone. His goals and his career had been our main focus, my life so totally enmeshed in his that I did not know who I was or what my goals were. It was a very scary time.

My decision was to go back to school and earn a master's degree in elementary education. I had taught on an emergency certificate in the late 1950s with only three years of college, then later went back and got my undergraduate degree in elementary education.

I will never forget that first year of teaching. I was painfully young, terribly inexperienced. However, I discovered something about myself. I know now that I must have been born an affective teacher. I remember looking at my students and knowing there was more to teaching than just reading, writing, and arithmetic. I taught children!

When the children left me that first year, I said a prayer, asking God's forgiveness for failing to do what I should have done for them, or for doing what I should not have done. And, I never wanted to see them again! I felt like a failure. Several years later, when a lady approached me and asked, "Are you Mrs. Hartline who taught at Kingsbury Elementary?" I confessed that I was. She said, "My daughter was in your class. She was a breech birth and walked with a limp. You taught her it was okay. It was one of the happiest years of her school life." My philosophy of working with children was strengthened and reaffirmed by her statement.

The late 1960s was an exciting time to be in graduate school. The work of Carl Rogers, Abraham Maslow, Sidney Simon, William Glasser, and many others was making an impact. The terms "self-actualization" and "wellness theory" caught my attention. I began to read and study, searching for my own identity. In the months following my husband's death I found Viktor Frankl's *Man's Search for Meaning*. I read that if you have a reason for living you can stand anything. I looked at my little girl, who was only six years old at the time, and thought of my love of teaching. I thought of the young man who had been my husband for fourteen years. I thought of the partnership we had forged in those years—our hopes, our dreams. I could not let them die. I vowed that I would rebuild—for my daughter and for me. My faith in God and learning to believe in myself made it possible. I am grateful to all the people from whom I have learned and grown. They are many, beginning with Dr. Fred Mills of Edge Institute in Phoenix, Arizona, Dr. William Glasser, Dr. Sidney Simon,

Dr. Virginia Satir, Dr. Edward Ford, Dr. Muriel James, Dr. Valo Palomares, Dr. Gerry Alberson, Dr. Jack Canfield, and Dr. Robert Schuller. I cannot begin to thank all of the authors of books I have read for the contribution they have made to my life and to my study of self-esteem.

Two years after my husband's death, we relocated to Phoenix, Arizona, I with a brand new master's degree. My first teaching assignment was a fourth-grade class. I was still dealing with my problem of identity, reading and attending seminars in the area of self-esteem. I began to think how much better it would be for my students to have some handles on living much earlier in life than I did. I started an interest center on self-esteem. I called it the "Me Unit." The study of self became a viable part of our curriculum.

I am indebted to many people who began to produce self-esteem materials in the 1970s and on into the 1980s. One of my favorite activities was Dr. Sidney Simon's I.A.L.A.C. story. I remember the thrill of receiving the Magic Circle training from Gerry and Valo Palomares.

Today it is wonderful to see people producing materials and leading workshops in self-esteem. I applaud them all. Now I teach classes and workshops for teachers, and count myself most fortunate to spend my days in work in which I so deeply believe. As I look back over my career, a large part of which has been spent with students, I am reminded of these lines from David Melton's book, *Although the Day Is Not Mine to Give, I'll Show You the Morning Sun:*

> *Take my hand, my child,*
> *And we will explore the land.*
> *I will tell you all that I know,*
> *And you will show me the secrets of*
>   *the heart.*
> *It may not be a fair exchange,*
> *But it is all that I have to give.*

These students have greatly enriched my life. They gave so much to me, and I gave them what I had to give. I hope the lessons have served them well in life. I hope my sharing with you through this book will enrich your life and those of your students.

Jo Ellen Hartline

ACKNOWLEDGMENTS

About ten years ago a lady followed me out of a workshop I had just conducted. She asked if I had written anything down. I had not. However, with her encouragement and belief in me, my first book was published in 1982, and now this revision. That lady was Joey Tanner of Zephyr Press, and I am greatly indebted to her.

I want to thank my daughter, Melody Jo Hartline-Buckner, for continuing to support my efforts with her artwork.

Thank you, Ed Rosenberg, for teaching me how to use the computer while I was doing the revision. Thank you, Brenda Ainley, for editing the work.

Lastly, I thank all of my students, children and adults, for sharing their lives with me in this journey of growth and discovery. You have inspired, enriched, and blessed my life.

1

INTRODUCTION

If you treat an individual as he is, that's all that he will be.
Only if you treat him as he ought to be, will he have a chance
to become what he ought to be or could.

—400-year-old quote

When I teach classes for teachers, two of my favorite activities to begin are "My Board of Directors" and "The Ten Most Important Lessons in Life." I learned the "Board of Directors" activity from Constance H. Dembrowsky at the First National Conference on Self-Esteem in Los Angeles a couple of years ago. Connie has developed curriculum materials for junior and senior high school students. This information is listed in the Resources chapter of this book. "Chairman of the Board" is also a strategy given in *Meeting Yourself Halfway,* by Dr. Sidney Simon, also listed in the Resources chapter. I learned "The Ten Most Important Lessons in Life" from my training in Magic Circle.*

My Board of Directors

While I play "Wind Beneath My Wings"** I have my students list people who sit on their "Board of Directors." These are their heroes—people who have made significant contributions to their lives. Then the class talks about these people and what they have contributed. Responses go like this: unconditional love, a belief in myself, a work ethic, a value system, etc. And these things came from their parents, husbands, wives, children, friends, and many times from teachers. I read to them the passage from Dr. William Glasser's

* Palomares and Associates, P. O. Box 1517, Spring Valley, California 92077.
** Bette Midler, Atlantic Recording Corporation, 75 Rockefeller Plaza, New York, New York 10019.

book *Control Theory in the Classroom,* in which he dedicates the book to his sixth-grade English teacher. Dr. Glasser says, "Perhaps this incident [being accepting of him] sparked my interest in how the mind works. I like to think so, but most of all I like to think that she loved me."

Then I ask the teachers if they hope that their students would someday put them on their Board of Directors. As teachers we hope to make a positive, lasting impact on the lives of our students.

I have the teachers list their most important lessons in life. I begin by saying one of my most important lessons was learning to deal with my parent's divorce when I was six years old. I have teachers share lessons they have learned. These lessons include losing a job, dealing with illness (their own or someone's close to them), learning that life is not fair, learning that we must face the consequences of our actions, learning to deal with losses, etc. Most said they had never had any training with such problems; that any help usually came through family, or through a church affiliation. Most said it just came from "the school of hard knocks."

I tell them the story of Rick Little, the founder of Quest, and his determination to teach lessons on life skills to young people. (His wonderful curriculum materials are listed in the Resources chapter of this book.) I tell the story of how I embarked on my study of self-esteem and then wanted to share my findings with my students.

The teachers and I talk of the need to convey these lessons to children as young as kindergarten age. My area of concentration has been to put the study of self into the school curriculum through an interest center in the classroom. My plan is laid out for you in the chapter of this book entitled "Method of Teaching Self-Esteem in the Classroom."

In this book I demonstrate the need for teaching self-esteem. In a survey in *Childhood Education,* November/ December 1984, Survey of Community Expectations—Top-Rated Goals (Elementary), parents listed six things they want for their children. One goal was developing pride in work and a feeling of self-worth; another was to develop good character and self-respect. I believe the third goal, which was to develop a desire for learning now and in the future, also relates to self-esteem. Not only teachers but parents feel students need lessons in life skills.

This book is not just a method of teaching self-esteem and a listing of support materials, but rather it is my attempt to share a philosophy of living and teaching based on the belief that each child is special and unique and should be treated with great respect and dignity. The school has had to assume more and more responsibility for the whole child. With the present-day knowledge explosion, children are growing up in a world in which there are no job descriptions of the roles some of them may fill in life. We can no longer concentrate simply on stuffing facts into their heads. We must give them some "handles" for living, decision making, and problem solving. Why not start with very young children and help them learn things about themselves, which will, hopefully, enable them to grow up to be happy, well-adjusted adults?

I believe this business of building self-esteem is the very foundation of education and life. How a person regards him or herself has a bearing on every area of life and how he or she lives it. Children need to know they are loved and accepted as they are—that they have worth. There is research to show a high correlation between school achievement and self-esteem, motivation and self-esteem, and teacher expectation and student achievement. However, I feel the most important reason for teachers to be concerned with enhancing the self-esteem of their students is to help students to achieve self-actualization, to reach their full potential, and to become happy, well-adjusted, productive, responsible adults. Ashley Montague, *On Being Human,* put it so well when he said, "For all the knowledge in the world is worse than useless if it is not humanely understood and humanely used. An intelligence that is not humane is the worst thing in the world."

Psychologist Dr. Abraham Maslow challenged us to study wellness and to build on strengths, working toward prevention of mental and emotional problems. His work on self-actualization has much to say to us in education. Frank G. Goble in *The Third Force, the Psychology of Abraham Maslow,* said Maslow loosely defined self-actualization as "the full use and exploitation of talent, capacities, potentialities, etc. Such people seem to be fulfilling themselves and doing the best that they are capable of doing."

It is far easier to implement preventive programs in our classrooms than to reap the havoc of adults who fill prisons and mental institutions. There are many ways that we can help students build upon their strengths, help them to learn more about themselves and like themselves, and help them to reach their full potential physically, mentally, emotionally, and spiritually. Perhaps, if we do a good job of teaching students to like themselves, some of the problems we have with drugs, school dropouts, teenage pregnancy, child abuse, vandalism, crime, and the pure waste of human potential can be minimized. I feel we should offer our young people information and techniques that will enable them to better understand themselves and others. This takes nothing away from the students academically; it only enhances the learning process.

Abraham Maslow's Hierarchy of Needs

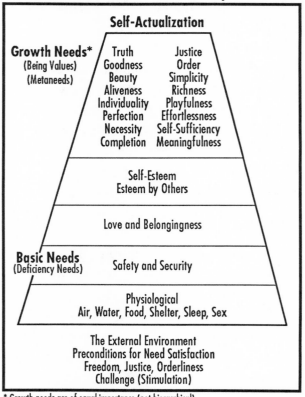

* Growth needs are of equal importance (not hierarchical)

School should be a happy place. A classroom should be beautifully and colorfully decorated. School should be a place where a child feels success and is accepted. I envision all children coming to school where teachers are their friends. If a lost friend asked for directions, you would not point to the long way around and confuse him or her. Rather, you would gently take that person by the hand and show the way. "Teacher" too many times denotes only authority, rules, and regulations. Our size is enough to be intimidating to a small child. If we could see the whole school through the eyes of the children, we might move a little more slowly toward them, speak a little more softly, listen a little more closely, and understand a great deal more. If we would treat each child as we would wish others to treat our own, it could make a big difference. Prudence Dyer, in "Love in Curriculum," *Theory Into Practice,* vol. 8, no. 2, April 1969, said, "Teaching children to love is the ideal—a possible dream—if we as teachers first love children." Students learn about love by experiencing respect and love from their teachers. "Teaching children to love is possible if we can provide an appropriate atmosphere and a curriculum through which mutual love and respect can flourish."

How do we become better teachers and have classrooms where children grow and blossom? We continue to learn. We read, we study, we take classes, we stay open to new ideas, we hold on to that which is good and add new things as we grow and learn. We never take the stance that we know it all, that we have "arrived." As a reading specialist I have learned along the way that the more I understand about reading problems, the more there is to learn, and what a complex process learning to read is.

This book was developed out of my own personal philosophy of education. In it I will be sharing with you some ideas of how I taught self-esteem in a classroom. I drew from many sources. Some of the materials I found most valuable to draw upon were *One Hundred Ways to Enhance Self-Esteem in the Classroom,* by Jack Canfield and Harold Wells, and *Self-Esteem, a Classroom Affair,* vols. 1 & 2, by Michele Borba. Borba's latest book, *Esteem Builders,* will provide you with many activities. Jack Canfield's *Self-Esteem in the Classroom: A Curriculum Guide* and Robert Reasoner's *Building Self-Esteem* are excellent curriculum guides. In his guide, Robert Reasoner has taken some building blocks for development of self-esteem, i.e., establishing a sense of security, developing a sense of identity or self-concept, creating a sense of belonging, developing a sense of purpose, and achieving a sense of personal competence, and developed units for teaching these areas in the classroom. The Quest program now provides curriculum guides and training for K-12. *Tribes,* by Jeanne Gibbs, gives many affective cooperative learning activities to be carried out in the classroom.

One of my favorite activities is Magic Circle. This process is an excellent bonding exercise to bring children together as a class. It is also wonderful for oral language development and for teaching communication skills, as well as to enhance the self-esteem of students. The Magic Circle association has a commitment to produce a wealth of materials to support this process. One of their latest publications is *Just Say I Know How,* produced by Innerchoice Publishing, which was designed to teach lessons in self-esteem to combat drug use.

These aids are all listed in the Resources chapter of this book, along with many others, to help you become aware of how much is available to help you design a program for your own classroom.

I would like to point out two other resources. "A Generation at Risk," available from PTV Publications, P. O. Box 701, Kent, Ohio 44240, is an excellent video, showing programs that are making an impact on troubled teens. It focuses on the problems of teens and some successful ways to deal with the problems. The emphasis is on building self-esteem.

A recently published report by the state of California demonstrates that self-esteem may well be the unifying concept to re-frame American problem solving.*

This comprehensive report of a three-year study deals with the family, education and academic failure, drug and alcohol abuse, crime and violence, poverty and chronic welfare dependency, and the workplace. It relates self-esteem and its implications to each of these areas. Findings are given and recommendations are made. This publication, entitled *Toward a State of Esteem, the Final Report of the California Task Force to Promote Self-Esteem and Personal and Social Responsibility,* and a 200-page appendix in a separate volume, contain much valuable information to help us move toward making the teaching of self-esteem a viable part of the school curriculum.

You are unique and special, and I hope my book will be just a springboard for you to develop your own unit on self-esteem. I wish you well as you undertake the challenge of meeting the needs of your students in all areas of their lives.

A great Teacher admonished us to love others as we love ourselves. Maybe, as we learn to love ourselves, we will find more love and acceptance of others and thus bring about a better life for all.

We can think of ourselves not as teachers, but as gardeners. "A gardener does not grow flowers"; he tries to give them what he thinks will help them grow, and they grow by themselves. A child's mind, like a flower, is a living thing. We can't make it grow by sticking things onto it any more than we can make a flower grow by gluing on leaves and petals. All we can do is surround the growing mind with what it needs for growing and have faith that it will take what it needs and grow.

John Holt

* Available from the Bureau of Publications, California State Department of Education, P. O. Box 271, Sacramento, California 95802-0271.

2
BOOK TALK

Much of my knowledge in self-esteem has come from reading and studying books on my own. My reading is very eclectic. I read EVERYTHING. Then I pick and choose according to how a particular book or author fits into my personal value system or philosophy of living. Some books and authors have added more to my growth and knowledge than others, but I have found value in all of the books. Sometimes I am asked to prioritize the books for one just beginning a study of self-esteem. For this reason I have added a "book talk" at the beginning of my self-esteem classes. I also do a book talk for another reason. It is hard to give away something you don't have. Teachers may need to work on their own self-esteem first in order to be good models for their students. Here are some good books for starters. All of these are listed in the Adult Bibliography at the end of this book.

First, I would point you to Dorothy Briggs' *Celebrate the Self*. You may already be familiar with her book *Your Child's Self-Esteem,* which has been so helpful to parents and teachers. *Celebrate*

the Self will help you get some insight into your own self-esteem.

Any books or tapes by Nathaniel Branden will give you much information on the psychology of self-esteem.

The Antecedents of Self-Esteem, by Stanley Coopersmith, is probably the most definitive study of self-esteem. If you are looking for research in self-esteem and its implications for working with students, this is the book.

The Third Force, by Frank G. Goble, is a digest of the psychology of Abraham Maslow.

Love, by Leo Buscaglia, is a favorite of mine. I encourage every teacher to read it. As an educator himself, Dr. Buscaglia appeals to us to recognize the feeling world of the student.

Self-Esteem, by Matthew McKay and Patrick Fanning, is a very complete study on the subject.

I particularly like a book entitled *Women and Self-Esteem,* by Linda Tschirhart Sanford and Mary Ellen Donovan. I also recommend this book for men. A particular point that I find most helpful is this: None of us had all our needs met as we grew up, nor did our parents. But we can find "brothers and sisters" (friends, significant others) who will help us find our way. The responsibility lies with us, not with others, to get our needs met.

Wayne Dyer's books and tapes are also helpful in giving us techniques on dealing with issues in life. His book *Your Erroneous Zones,* is particularly good for helping to let go of guilt feelings.

The Road Less Traveled, by Scott Peck, is excellent for its blend of psychology and the spiritual. He points out that until we accept that life is made up of challenges and that we need to bring our best to solving these challenges, we will not find happiness. There is tremendous joy and inner satisfaction once we arrive at this conclusion and accept responsibility for our lives. I once heard Dr. Sidney Simon say, "Life ain't no ride on no pink duck!" Sometimes as I read the newspaper and listen to the news, I feel the world must be looking for that "pink duck" rather than looking within to find the answers and solve the problems. I feel the avoidance of this is sometimes reflected in our society by escapism into alcohol and drugs.

Man's Search for Meaning, by Viktor Frankl, has made a profound impact on my life. The first part of the book is autobiographical. His logotherapy appealed to me when I had to get on with my life after my husband died. To paraphrase, he said, It has happened; it is over and done; all the crying and raving will not change things; now square your shoulders and face tomorrow. He states: "Limits of choice are set by heredity and environmental influence, but within these prescribed limits we always have a remaining area of freedom to choose the ATTITUDE we will take toward the present condition." I find that greatly empowering. In any circumstance, there are choices. This knowledge has greatly enriched my life, and I work with my students to show them that they always have choices. They need to know this when life gets rough.

In *Believe in the God Who Believes in You,* Dr. Robert Schuller relates each of the Ten Commandments to self-esteem.

Most of us know Judith Viorst from the wonderful children's book of *Alexander,* but she does write for adults. Her book *Necessary Losses* is wonderful in teaching us how to deal with the losses that we all have in life. "Dear Abby" printed a beautiful story by Emily Perl Kingsley. It was written about giving birth to a child with disabilities, but it could apply to every aspect of one's life. Ms. Kingsley likened life to going on a trip but being booked on the wrong tour and ending up at the wrong destination. As long as we keep looking back, we miss the beauty of the country around us. It is the same with life. We miss our own beauty and our own blessings if we stay hung up in what might have been. In the movie *Old Gringo*, there was a line that said, "Life is an awkward rough draft." Letting go of these losses enables us to make the most of what is. The pain may be always tucked away in a corner of our hearts, but we need to get on with living today. A phrase I learned from Dr. William Glasser helps me get a proper perspective on things when I'm dealing with one of life's adversities: "In the great scheme of things, this was going to happen today." Sometimes one can smile, even chuckle, when viewing things this way.

And speaking of Dr. Glasser, I would highly recommend his book *Control Theory in the Classroom.* He writes about why many capable students make little or no effort to learn. He states that when they start school, students have "pictures" in their heads that they can become learners. If these "pictures" are erased, for whatever reason, they are very difficult to put back. As educators we must keep the pictures there.

Hide or Seek, by Dr. James Dobson, gives some very practical techniques for building self-esteem in children. *For the Love of Children,* by Edward Ford and Steven Englund, is a book I highly recommend for teachers and parents for excellent ideas on discipline and teaching responsibility. *The Secret of Staying in Love,* by John Powell, gives great insight into learning to love yourself, with some very practical exercises at the end of the book—exercises that would make excellent journal writing topics. Two books on codependency which deal a lot with self-esteem are *Codependent No More* and *Beyond Codependency and Getting Better All the Time,* by Melody Beattie.

John Bradshaw's *Healing the Shame That Binds You* is a powerful book. He states: "Healthy shame is an emotion which signals us about our limits and keeps us grounded. Toxic shame is experienced as the all-pervasive sense that 'I am flawed and defective as a human being.' It is a state of being. Guilt does not reflect directly upon one's identity or diminish one's sense of personal worth. In guilt the possibility of repair exists and learning and growth are promoted. Guilt is a painful feeling of regret and responsibility for one's actions. Shame is a painful feeling about oneself as a person." John Bradshaw has done a tremendous amount of research into shame and its implications for us as human beings struggling with these feelings.

When Smart People Fail, by Carole Hyatt and Linda Gottlieb, helps put failure in its proper perspective. They say that a failure is an event in a series of events in life. It does not define us forever and ever. *Do What You Love, the Money Will Follow,* by Marsha Sinetar, teaches us to find the work in life from which we will gain the most joy and satisfaction. If you like yourself, you will believe that you deserve to have work that makes you happy. This gives full rein to your creativity. Being happy in one's work is important to one's self-esteem.

A medical book I always recommend is *Getting Well Again,* by Stephanie Matthews-Simonton, Dr. Carl Simonton, and James L. Creighton. This book has to do with the psychological effect of physical illness. It is a book about keeping well, mentally and physically. Another book is *Love, Medicine and Miracles,* by Dr. Bernie S. Siegel. This is a wonderful book of hope. Two very inspiring books by Walter Anderson are *Courage Is a Three-Letter Word,* telling us to say YES to life, and *The Greatest Risk of All,* telling us to take risks in our lives and be all we can be.

I love using stories to make a point, and Paul Harvey's *The Rest of the Story* is an excellent resource. These stories are good to use with your students to inspire and motivate them. As teachers we will all be inspired by Eliot Wigginton's book, *Sometimes a Shining Moment: The Foxfire Experience*. This is about a teacher in the Appalachian region who, with his students, publishes the *Foxfire* books. He has helped his students build healthy self-esteem by becoming productive human beings. His standards for his students instill a desire within them to be the best they can be.

I hope my "book talk" has whetted your appetite to do some reading in self-esteem and related areas. I have found books very healing in my life, and I offer them to you for the same reason.

3
SOME OF MY FAVORITE THINGS

If I can say that I am shy
It seems you always pass me by.
Funny how it seems to be
Self-fulfilling prophecy.

If I can say you're a bad person,
I can almost see you worsen,
Funny how my words for you
Have a way of coming true.

If you say that I am selfish
I feel hard as any shellfish.
I can almost guarantee
You won't get a thing from me.

Strange how your words for me
Make me into what you see.
Label, label there's no way
To win this game today.

—L. Eugene Arnold

THE SPECIAL STORY OF MISS THOMPSON

I know of a schoolteacher named Miss Thompson. Every year when she met her new students she would say, "Boys and girls, I love you all the same. I have no favorites." Of course, she wasn't being completely truthful. Teachers do have favorites and, what is worse, most teachers have students that they just don't like.

Teddy Stallard was a boy that Miss Thompson just didn't like, and for good reason. He just didn't seem interested in school. There was a deadpan, blank expression on his face and his eyes had a glassy, unfocused appearance. When she spoke to Teddy, he always answered in monosyllables. His clothes were musty and his hair was unkempt. He wasn't an attractive boy and he certainly wasn't likable.

Whenever she marked Teddy's papers, she got a certain perverse pleasure out of putting X's next to the wrong answers, and when she put the F's at the top of the papers, she always did it with a flair. She should have known better; she had Teddy's records and she knew more about him than she wanted to admit. The records read:

1st Grade: Teddy shows promise with his work and attitude, but poor home situation.

2nd Grade: Teddy could do better. Mother is seriously ill. He receives little help at home.

3rd Grade: Teddy is a good boy, but too serious. He is a slow learner. His mother died this year.

4th Grade: Teddy is very slow, but well-behaved. His father shows no interest.

Christmas came and the boys and girls in Miss Thompson's class brought her Christmas presents. They piled their presents on her desk and crowded around to watch her open them. Among the presents, there was one from Teddy Stallard. She was surprised that he had brought her a gift, but he had. Teddy's gift was wrapped in brown paper and was held together with Scotch tape. On the paper were written the simple words, "For Miss Thompson from Teddy." When she opened Teddy's present, out fell a gaudy rhinestone bracelet with half the stones missing, and a bottle of cheap perfume.

The other boys and girls began to giggle and smirk over Teddy's gifts, but Miss Thompson at least had enough sense to silence them by immediately putting on the bracelet and putting some of the perfume on her wrist. Holding her wrist up for the other children to smell, she said,

"Doesn't it smell lovely?" And the children, taking their cue from the teacher, readily agreed with "oo's" and "ah's."

At the end of the day, when school was over and the other children had left, Teddy lingered behind. He slowly came over to her desk and said softly, "Miss Thompson . . . Miss Thompson, you smell just like my mother . . . and her bracelet looks real pretty on you, too. I'm glad you liked my presents."

When Teddy left, Miss Thompson got down on her knees and asked God to forgive her.

The next day when the children came to school, they were welcomed by a new teacher. Miss Thompson had become a different person. She was no longer just a teacher; she had become an agent of God. She was now a person committed to loving her children and doing things for them that would live on after her. She helped all the children, but especially the slow ones, and especially Teddy Stallard. By the end of that school year, Teddy showed dramatic improvement. He had caught up with most of the students and was even ahead of some.

She didn't hear from Teddy for a long time. Then one day, she received a note that read:

Dear Miss Thompson:
I wanted you to be the first to know. I will be graduating second in my class.
Love,
Teddy Stallard

Four years later, another note came:

Dear Miss Thompson:
They just told me I will be graduating first in my class. I wanted you to be the first to know. The university has not been easy, but I liked it.
Love,
Teddy Stallard

And, four years later:

Dear Miss Thompson:
As of today, I am Theodore Stallard, M.D. How about that? I wanted you to be the first to know. I am getting married next month, the 27th to be exact. I want you to come and sit where my mother would sit if she were alive. You are the only family I have now; Dad died last year.
Love,
Teddy Stallard

Miss Thompson went to that wedding and sat where Teddy's mother would have sat. She deserved to sit there; she had done something for Teddy that he could never forget.*

LOVE'S INSIGHT

"The poor thing!" That was my immediate reaction to my first glimpse of Nancy (not her real name). Her nose seemed too large for her thin little face and her mouth hung open strangely as she watched the stage performance in the school auditorium. While the other students laughed, Nancy showed no

* Anthony Campolo, *Who Switched the Price Tags?* (Waco, Texas: Word Books, 1986), pp. 69-72. Used by permission.

emotion. She seemed withdrawn, remote, dull, as well as unattractive.

Later in the faculty room I inquired who the new fourth-grader was.

"Oh, you must mean Nancy," a young teacher said. Her family just moved up here from the South and Nancy doesn't seem to understand our northern accents very well." I shook my head sadly. The child had a lot of handicaps, it seemed.

Busy with other things, I put Nancy out of my mind. But later that day, coming out of my office, I noticed a man and woman standing in the hall. They were apparently watching a child approaching behind me, and I was struck by the expressions of love and pride on their faces.

I turned to see which child they were awaiting with such happy anticipation. It was Nancy! She was hurrying toward them, smiling joyfully, every feature reflecting the uncritical love that was there waiting for her. And suddenly, seeing Nancy through the eyes of her father and mother, I found myself loving that little girl, because her parents were right—she was cute, she was appealing; the sparkle in her eyes revealed intelligence and humor.

The next months were to prove that Nancy was indeed a very bright child. By the time the school year ended, she was a happy, poised, popular little girl.

That afternoon in the hall I learned an invaluable lesson: to look at every child through the eyes of the person who loves him or her most, just as our own Heavenly Father regards each one of us—with patience and understanding and love and without the preconceived notions that can come from looking only at the outside.*

I have spent most of my teaching career in an inner-city school district. I have had people ask me if it was not discouraging working with these students, because I was up against such odds. There have been times when I have wondered if it was worth it. Did I make a difference? I have attended the funeral of one of my students who was murdered, another who was accidentally shot by his brother, and have watched students later go to prison or die of drug-related problems. But I have also had students who have gone on to high school and graduated and continued on to college. During the period when I was working so intensively with junior high students with reading problems and also doing lessons on self-esteem with them, I heard a speaker who brought the whole situation into proper perspective for me. He said to put your energy into the effort, not the outcome. My job was to be prepared for those students every day and give them the best I had, and then to let it go, probably never to know the outcome. Someone once wrote to me after I had written an article in *Today's Education* (N.E.A.) and said, "Teachers never hear the applause." So we just have to believe and give it our best shot every day and trust that our students will learn and use the lessons we teach. A teacher shared the following story with me, and I realized it could really be about teachers and their students. I share it with you so you will have it on those days you are discouraged and feel you do not make a difference. YOU DO!

IT MAKES A DIFFERENCE

A well-known author and poet was working and vacationing on the southern coast of Spain. One morning, very early, he was walking along the beach—the sun was just rising. While enjoying the beauty about him, he glanced down the beach and saw a lone figure dancing about. Fascinated by this other person celebrating the day that was about to dawn, he moved closer. As he came nearer, he realized that the young man was not dancing, but in one graceful movement was picking objects up from the beach and tossing them into the sea. As he approached the young man, he saw that the objects were starfish.

"Why in the world are you throwing starfish into the water?" "If the starfish are still on the beach when the tide goes out and the sun rises higher in the sky, they will die," replied the young man as he continued tossing them out to the sea.

"That's ridiculous! There are thousands of miles of beach and millions of starfish. You can't really believe that what you're doing could possibly make a difference!"

The young man picked up another starfish, paused thoughtfully, and remarked as he tossed it out into the waves, "It makes a difference to this one."*

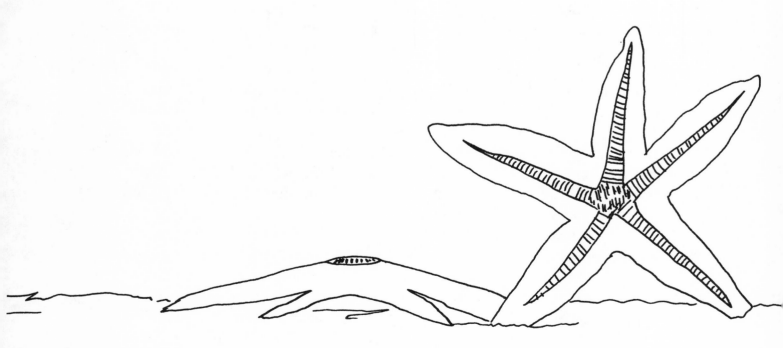

* Reprinted from *Animal News,* Animal Humane Society of Hennepin County and the Minnesota Network for Animal Concerns. *Animal News* is no longer in publication, but permission was obtained from the former editor to use this story.

4

SOME QUESTIONS ABOUT TEACHING SELF-ESTEEM

"What's the use of a book," thought Alice, "without pictures or conversation?"

—*Alice in Wonderland,*
Lewis Carroll

Won't the students be on an ego trip if you teach them to like themselves?

No, egotism is the same problem as feelings of inferiority. People who feel good about themselves will not be coming from either of these extremes. The student who says loudly, "I am the greatest," and walks all over everyone has just as much of a problem with self-esteem as the student who says, "I am not good at everything." They both need help in developing good self-esteem. Jack R. Frymier in an article entitled "Issues in Perspective" (*Theory Into Practice,* vol. 15, no. 1, pp. 23-30) states: "There are hundreds and hundreds of research studies in social psychology which dramatize and demonstrate very clearly that the concept and attitude towards others is rooted in concept of self. It takes people who feel good about themselves to have the strength to relate positively to other people."

There was a rise in the sixties of what has been termed the "Me" generation. The philosophy of "do your own thing" prevailed. I feel this is a very irresponsible philosophy; however, I do not think the sixties gave birth to this concept. It was more openly flaunted and accepted. There have always been selfish, self-centered people, and probably always will be. I see children hurt by this philosophy. My belief in enhancing the self-esteem of students is a very responsible one. There are basic values that are common to all of us. I believe success in achieving these basic values for all people depends upon our ability to like and accept ourselves and thereby learn tolerance and understanding of others.

When do we teach self-esteem? Will there be a special period once a week when we study self-esteem?

The philosophy behind enhancing the self-esteem of students permeates the whole day whether you are teaching math, social studies, or reading. The concepts should be evident in a humane classroom at all times. However, by teaching self-esteem through an interest center, you are assured of working it into the curriculum. Many of the activities in the ME unit focus on the skills you teach in the course of a day, i.e., writing, reading, listening, literature, communication skills, etc. How you use the interest center and how much time you spend with the unit is entirely up to you.

All of this sounds great, and I know my students need this, but when do I teach reading, writing, and arithmetic?

I contend that if you spend some quality time at the beginning of the year building rapport with the class and creating a humane environment where all children can experience success, you are going to get more academics out of the students than ever before. I believe if you invest time in Magic Circle, journal writing, having an interest center on self-esteem, reading to your students, showing and discussing special films with them, and sharing yourself with your students and allowing them to share themselves with you, then you are going to have happier students, a more productive class, fewer discipline problems, and a teacher who is not worn out at the end of the day. Howard L. Millman in an article "We Are People, Not Machines" (*Theory Into Practice,* vol. 15, no. 5, pp. 341-46) says: "People are capable of achieving more and creating more when they feel good about themselves." Richard L. Sartore in

an article entitled, "Students and Suicide: An Interpersonal Tragedy" (*Theory Into Practice,* vol. 15, no. 5, pp. 337-39) says "Students who experience success in school have a good chance of succeeding in life . . . hence schools are responsible for instilling worthwhile identities in young people so that opportunities for success are increased." On the other hand, he says, "Only in school are students so definitely labeled failures . . . The academic environment, under certain circumstances, perpetuates a suicidal crisis."

Will I be able to hold high standards for achievement and behavior if we have a warm, fuzzy environment in the classroom?

Yes, yes, yes! This is not a "soft" stance toward teaching. It takes a lot of work, commitment, and dedication to teach in this manner. First, you have to be prepared with creative, relevant lessons with lots of extra challenge to meet the needs of all your students so they may all experience success. You have to set high standards and help your students to achieve. Your expectations in the area of achievement and behavior for your students are paramount to their success in these areas.

Academically, students will not feel good about themselves if they do not experience growth in subject matter. Students do not feel good about themselves if they cannot read and function in the real world.

We need to motivate students to reach their full potential. We need to teach them the difference between satisfaction and gratification. Satisfaction is defined as coming from within, having successful relationships with self and others, and pressing yourself to your highest potential. Satisfaction is earned by hard work and commitment. Gratification comes from without the self, has temporary lasting value, and is not earned. We need to strive toward intrinsic motivation as opposed to extrinsic motivation.

Undisciplined students are unhappy students. They want someone to care enough to turn them around. They have no respect for a teacher who looks the other way and refuses to deal with the problem. Disciplining students takes time. We need to take the time, because we value human potential. We have the right to expect parents to help us solve the discipline problems of their children. All of us need to work together for the good of the child.

If you really achieve a humane environment in your classroom, you should have students who are achieving academically and who are relating well to self and others. Your discipline problems should be way down. At least now you should have time to invest in those students who seem to have more trouble with self-control than others. In such an atmosphere and climate, other students should be able to be supportive of you and their classmates as you work through problems in the classroom.

"Maybe the way I see others is the way I see myself."

5

DEFINITIONS

"Someone's opinion of you does not have to become your reality."

—Les Brown
Motivational Speaker

Self-esteem is defined as the way people feel about themselves. Self-concept or self-image is defined as the ideas or beliefs people have about themselves.

Dr. Nathaniel Branden in *Honoring the Self* states:

Self-esteem is the reputation we acquire with ourselves. Self-esteem is the integrated sum of self-confidence and self-respect.

Self-concept pertains to an individual's ideas, beliefs, and images concerning his or her (real or imagined) traits and characteristics,liabilities and assets, limitations and capabilities. It is wider than self-esteem; it contains self-esteem as one of its components. We may think of self-esteem as a circle enclosed within the wider circle of self-concept. Or we may think of self-esteem as the evaluative component of self-concept.

Dr. Robert Schuller in *Self-Esteem, the New Reformation* states:

Self-esteem is the human hunger for the divine dignity that God intended to be our emotional birthright as children created in His image.

Dr. Maxwell Maltz in *Psycho-Cybernetics: A New Way to Get More Out of Life* states:

Self-image is our own conception of the "sort of person I am." It has been built up by our own beliefs about ourselves. Most of these beliefs about ourselves have unconsciously been formed from our past experiences, our successes and failures, our humiliations, our triumphs, and the way other people have reacted to us, especially in early childhood. From all of these we mentally constructed a "self" (or a picture of a self). Once an idea or belief about ourselves goes into this picture it comes "true," as far as we personally are concerned. We do not question its validity, but proceed to act upon it just as if it were true. All of our actions, feelings, behavior—even your abilities—are always consistent with this self-image. The self-image is a "premise," a base, or a foundation upon which your entire personality, your behavior, and even your circumstances are built. The self-image can be changed. The self-conception must be changed.

Dr. Virginia Satir in *Peoplemaking* states:

Self-worth is the feelings and ideas one has about himself. In my many years of teaching young children, treating families of all economic and social levels, training people from all walks of life—from all the day-to-day experiences of my professional and personal living, I am convinced that the crucial factor in what happens both inside people and between people is the picture of individual worth that each person carries around with him—his self-worth. I am convinced that there are no genes to carry the feeling of worth. It is learned.

Dr. Dorothy Corkille Briggs in *Your Child's Self-Esteem* states:

Self-esteem is how a person feels about himself. It is his over-all judgment of himself—how much he likes his particular person. High self-esteem is not a noisy conceit. It is a quiet sense of self-respect, a feeling of self-worth. When you have it deep inside you, you're glad you're you. With high self-esteem you don't waste time and energy impressing others; you already know you have value. Strong self-respect is based on two main convictions: "I am lovable" ("I matter and have value because I exist") and "I am worthwhile" ("I can handle myself and my environment with competence; I know I have something to offer others"). She further states in *Celebrate Your Self—Enhancing Your Own Self-Esteem:*

Your self-image—who you think you are—is literally a package you put together from how others have seen and treated you and from your conclusions as you compared yourself to others. Your sense of identity is the end result of the interaction between your uniqueness and how others have reacted to it. It is the package you call "Me." But it does not tell me about your Real Self. For most of us, "Know thyself" means "Know what important others thought of you." It is never who you are that hangs you up, but rather who you think you are. Your self-image is learned; your real self is given.

Stanley Coopersmith in *Antecedents of Self-Esteem* states:

Self-esteem is the self-evaluation which the individual makes and customarily maintains with regard to himself; it expresses an attitude of approval or disapproval and indicates the extent to which the individual believes himself to be capable, significant, successful, and worthy.

Dr. Fred Mills in *Increasing Human Effectiveness* states:

Self-esteem is an emotion. It is the degree to which we consciously, or unconsciously, like or accept ourselves, in spite of our weaknesses or human frailties. It's how warm, friendly, and appreciative we actually feel toward ourselves. Our self-image is the picture we have of ourselves in our subconscious: and our self-esteem is the corresponding feeling we have, our self-love.

A healthy self-esteem says, "I am appropriate to life. I belong here. I have value and worth, and I can handle the challenges which life hands to me."

6

THE IMPORTANCE OF TEACHING SELF-ESTEEM

Maybe the essence of education is not to stuff you with facts
but to help you discover your uniqueness, to teach you how to
develop it, and then to show you how to give it away.

—Leo Buscaglia from *Love*

There are many statistics available to point out the problems of students today, i.e., drugs, dropout problems, poverty, dysfunctional homes, gang problems, teen pregnancy, apathy on the part of our students, etc. One piece of research from a 1987 PBS Special, "Generation at Risk," states that

- One out of every four children will become a problem drinker in high school.
- An American teenager commits suicide every 90 minutes.
- One-fourth of our children will drop out of high school.
- Four out of every 10 girls will become pregnant before they leave their teens.

Research has concluded that there is a common character trait exhibited by the children who are involved in these findings. Ninety percent of them have low self-esteem. We know that programs developed to combat these problems must have a heavy component of self-esteem or they miss the mark.

We know from other research that the problems are now reaching as low as fourth-grade level. A *Weekly Reader* poll in 1983 found that one in four fourth-graders feel "some" to "a lot" of peer pressure to drink alcohol.

In *Children Today,* May-June 1987, it was reported that, if present trends continue, of a 40-member class graduating high school in the year 2000: two class members will give birth before graduation, eight will drop out of school, 11 will be unemployed after graduation, 15 will be living in poverty; by graduation 36 will have used alcohol, 17 will have tried marijuana and eight will have used cocaine, six will have run away from home, and one will have committed suicide.

A survey sponsored by health education groups and the Department of

Health and Human Services polled 11,000 eighth- and tenth-graders during the fall of 1987 from a nationally representative sample of 217 public and private schools. Dr. Robert E. Windom, assistant health secretary and head of the Public Health Service, called the results "somewhat dismaying." In some of the more startling findings, the study reported that 26 percent of the eighth-graders and 38 percent of the 10th-graders said they had had five or more drinks on one occasion during the two weeks preceding the survey. Also, 42 percent of the girls and 25 percent of the boys surveyed said they had "seriously thought" about committing suicide at some time in their lives. Nearly one girl in five and one boy in ten of the total survey said they had actually tried to commit suicide. There seemed to be a consistent pattern of hopelessness, of depression, in some of the responses.

When an article by Eileen Putnam of the Associated Press reported these findings in my local paper, a local talk-show host read it over the air and asked teenagers to call in. The ones who called painted a dreary picture. They said they had no role models. They saw corruption on every hand in every walk of life. They did not believe they would grow to be old; that we would go up in a nuclear war. Their philosophy seemed to be, "Eat, drink, and be merry for tomorrow we die." What astounded me was that none of them were looking inside themselves for answers. They wanted instant gratification and easy solutions. Was it frightening? You bet it was.

One state gave seniors a test to measure their writing/language skills. At the end of the test they were asked to write a paragraph. Psychologists were called in to review these writings. Many of the students wrote of their problems and frustrations.

As I read this I thought, Was this the only place these students had to vent these feelings?

Other research has shown that most children start school with high self-esteem, and then it diminishes as they progress through school. Many things happen to them along the way—at home, in the classrooms, on the playground, and in life in general. I once stepped inside a classroom of kindergarten students. As I stood with the teacher looking at the students, one little girl and I made eye contact. The next minute, she pushed her crayons back and approached me, pulling on my skirt. She said, "Teacher, I will sing a song for you." She threw back her little head and sang. As I looked into that child's face, I thought, May you always have a song to sing, and may you always feel that someone wants to hear your song.

Karen Horney, who has done extensive work in personality development theories, has shown that EVERYONE has strong drives to achieve competence and to gain approval. She states that children who know how to increase their powers, and how at the same time to gain the approval of adults and peers, develop stable, healthy personalities and are both effective and highly motivated. Eager to try and able to succeed, emotionally healthy children respond successfully to challenges and are motivated by their success to react positively to further challenge.

With this knowledge many people have set about to develop programs to teach students these skills. These programs provide ways to open children to a discussion of life that will help them to become informed, confident, and capable. There is hope, and it lies with us as educators to care enough to implement these programs.

A recent survey funded by the National Institute on Drug Abuse, a research arm of the Department of Health and Human Services, said that illegal drug use dropped last year among all three categories of young people surveyed and that casual use among high school seniors and college students is about half what it was a decade earlier. Health and Human Services secretary Louis Sullivan said that although the continued trend is good news, "too many people still use drugs," and he expressed concern about the level of alcohol and tobacco use in high schools. William Bennett, director of the Office of National Drug Control Policy, said the survey results are "very encouraging," but he added, "Now is precisely not the time to ease up on our efforts."

My observation may be very simplistic on this drug war situation. If there were not a need for people to escape, if they could face life squarely and responsibly, there would be no market for drugs. Let us try to give students the tools they need to face life honorably and courageously. And, just maybe, they—and all of us—could have a better quality of life.

I once watched the late Sammy Davis, Jr., on a talk show. He was laughing and sharing with the audience; then the host asked him about his drug problem. He became very sober. When asked what he had done to turn his life around, instead of mentioning a rehabilitation center, he smiled a wonderful smile as the camera panned in on his famous face and said, "I learned to love me."

In another special, taped in a rehabilitation center, a group gathered in a circle and shared their feelings. There was much pain among that small group. One man told of looking into a mirror and feeling for the first time that he belonged in life, that he was appropriate for life.

If we could teach children to learn to like and love themselves and to feel that they are appropriate to life, perhaps they would grow up to be happier, more responsible adults. Perhaps they could feel a sense of empowerment in their own destiny; perhaps the hopelessness that teenagers expressed in the earlier survey would not be a part of their lives.

Information is available to give us insight into what children need for success in life. A poll was conducted for *Family Circle* (April 5, 1988) by the Gallup Organization. The study compared childhood memories of extraordinarily successful people—and the parents who raised them—with the recollections of a control group of parents chosen at random from the general population, without regard to whether their children had achieved success in their chosen field. The 237 successful adults interviewed for the survey have reached the highest levels of distinction in politics, business, journalism, sports, entertainment, science, the arts, and the humanities. I am using this information for its implications in self-esteem.

These outstanding achievers received parental time rather than money. Respect for children's independence and individuality was emphasized, rather than force-fed lessons at any early age. Fathers of superachievers played a more active role in their youngsters' lives than other fathers. Parents of achievers spent more time simply talking with their children. These children were greatly interested in reading and there were significantly more books in the homes of the more successful group. These successful people were allowed more independence at an earlier age.

David Elkind, Ph.D., professor of child study and senior resident scholar at Tufts University, says there is ample evidence to support the finding that independence and free, unstructured time to pursue their own interests are critical factors in the development of children's talents. He says when children learn to read, they need time to explore books by themselves without a specific goal in mind. The comments of highly successful people bear out this point. One high-ranking politician said his mother had had great influence on his success by encouraging him to work harder in school and telling him he could do anything he wanted to do. The parents of these successful people saw their children as self-confident, handling crises well, being ambitious, having original ideas, setting their own goals, being curious, and taking risks. When asked who had exerted the greatest influence on their success, about one-fourth said their fathers, 17 percent

picked their fathers and mothers, 16 percent named their mothers only, and roughly 11 percent credited teachers.

Findings from this survey stated: (1) The important thing is the time that parents spend with children, not things that the parents buy for them. (2) Father is a very important part of a child's life. (3) Put children "in charge" so they can learn responsibility, gain confidence, and achieve a sense of accomplishment. (4) Set reasonable standards of behavior. Being rigidly strict creates children who can follow rules but not necessarily think for themselves. (5) Treat children with respect. Allow them their own interests and ambitions. This will boost their self-esteem and also show them how to respect other people. And don't forget the hugs and kisses, says Dr. T. Berry Brazelton, a child-development expert. Helping children feel good about themselves is one of the most valuable assets with which you can endow them.

Consider the four conditions of high self-esteem from *The Antecedents of Self-Esteem* by Stanley Coopersmith: (1) The child experiences full acceptance of thoughts, feelings, and the value of his or her being. (2) The child operates in a context of clearly defined and enforced limits that are fair, nonoppressive, and negotiable—but the child is not given unrestricted "freedom." (3) The child experiences respect for his or her dignity as a human being. (4) Parents themselves tend to enjoy a high level of self-esteem. Dr. Coopersmith stated, however, that there are virtually no parental patterns of behavior or parental attitudes that are common to all parents of children with high self-esteem. He also said that not all of these conditions are essential for the formation of high esteem, and the study suggested that combinations of the conditions are required. Some children emerge with high self-esteem no matter what happens to them.

Let's take a look at the research that is available and its implications for us as educators.

Dr. Maxwell Maltz made two important observations in his book *Psycho-Cybernetics.* First, all of your actions, feelings, behavior—even your abilities—are always consistent with your self-image. Second, the self-image can be changed. Dr. Maltz states that self-image is changed, for better or worse, not by intellect alone, nor by intellectual knowledge alone, but by "experiencing." It is not the child who has been taught about love but the child who has experienced love that grows into a healthy, happy, well-adjusted adult.

Prescott Lecky, one of the pioneers in self-image psychology, states in his book *Self-Consistency, A Theory of Personality,* that students who were failing in certain school subjects made great improvement when their self-concept changed. Then came a change in attitude toward the subject. Then there was success. These findings have much to say to us in education. Students need to experience success, and success will breed success. Teachers need to help them in this process.

Arthur Combs (*Perceiving, Behaving, Becoming,* 1962) in writing of the role of the school in self-concept stated: "What happens to the self in the course of schooling may be far more important than whatever else schools think they are teaching. Self-concept is a vital part of the learning process, and truly effective education must be humanistically oriented toward student self-concepts."

Neil Postman (*The School Book,* 1975) emphasizes the significant role of the school in relation to self-concept. He believes that schools must assume some responsibility for the emotional growth of children. Postman says he does not mean that schools should become psychiatric hospitals, but feels that many students have been "rendered intellectually ineffective and socially destructive by worry, dread, rage, hostility, and confusion." Public schools "cannot handle this problem by hiring a few guidance counselors." Postman feels that the study of one's own feelings must become a legitimate school activity, given at least the same importance as map-reading skills and spelling. He states, "We do know that when schools take the feeling-life of children seriously, children become less fearful, less diffident, less lost, and, as a consequence, more fully functioning human beings. They also become better learners."

Research shows a high correlation between positive self-concept and academic achievement and between negative self-concept and nonachievement or underachievement. Students who feel good about themselves and their ability to learn and be successful, tend to learn more, like school better, stay in school longer, and attend more regularly. (Purkey, 1970; Bloom,

1976; Brookover, 1977; Brookover, 1973; Rosenthal and Jacobson, 1968; Mayeske, 1968; Wylie, 1961; Epstein and McPartland, 1974.)

Students who believe they have the academic ability to succeed in specific subject areas, such as reading or math, tend to learn more. Students also learn more when they like the specific subject area. (Purkey, 1970; Bloom, 1976; Brookover, 1977.)

Students who feel that they are worthwhile human beings are better able to perform required work, are more eager to learn, more confident, more ambitious, and exhibit more mature behavior. They indicate a sense of belonging and need fewer favorable comments from other people. They believe they work hard and are generally polite and honest. (Purkey, 1970; Brookover, 1977; Epstein and McPartland, 1972, 1975; Rosenthal and Jacobson, 1968.)

Students under stress of failure perform at lower levels and suffer a lowered opinion of themselves and their academic abilities. The opposite is also true. Students who succeed do better work and feel better about themselves. (Purkey, 1970; *What Research Says,* 1973; McDill and Rigsby, 1973; McDill, Meyers and Rigsby, 1966; Brookover, 1977; McDill, Rigsby and Meyers, 1969.)

Students' feelings about themselves can be affected either positively or negatively by what they perceive is expected of them by friends, teachers, parents—the people who are important to them. Aspy and Roebuck (1976) found that teachers who provide high facilitative conditions (empathy, understanding,

congruence, genuineness, positive regard, respect) in the classroom can improve the academic achievement of their students. A sobering finding was that the students of teachers low in facilitative conditions might actually be retarded in their learning by this deficiency. Examples of other positive gains in students who have high facilitative teachers include: more adept use of higher cognitive processes such as problem solving, more positive self-concept than was found in other groups, more initiated behavior in the classroom, fewer discipline problems, and lower rates of absence from school.

The research of Rosenthal and Jacobson (1968) has found that when the teacher believes that students can achieve, the students appear to be more successful; when the teacher believes the students cannot achieve, their performance is influenced negatively. They summarized their study by stating that evidence strongly suggests that "children who are expected by their teachers to gain intellectually in fact do show greater intellectual gains after one year than do children of whom such gains are not expected."

Dr. Frances Bond, writing in the Allyn and Bacon Reading Newsletter, no. 5, states, "Empirical and experimental data indicate that many children who are retarded in reading have low self-regard. The relationship between self-concept and reading disability is not limited to extreme cases. Rather, the research on this relationship generally describes the disability in terms of one to two years below grade level."

With the critical reading problems

identified in this country, it would pay us to look at the research and the correlation between reading and self-esteem. Dr. George Spache in *Good Reading for the Disadvantaged Reader* (Garrard Publishing Company, 1975), devotes the first part of this book to self-concept and its relationship to reading. Dr. Spache quotes findings from research that declares that self-concept is shown to be more closely related to reading performance than intelligence itself. He further states that many studies of good readers show that they possess feelings of personal worth, personal freedom, and self-reliance and belonging. He says poor readers often feel discouraged and hopeless in their efforts to succeed in school.

Eda J. LeShan in an article, "Teaching (and Learning) Are Easier—If You Know How You Feel," *Today's Education*, February-March 1980, wrote of recording interviews with ex-convicts for a book on crime. They had all been troublemakers in school. They had never seen school as a safe place from the harshness of their experiences at home or on the streets. They could not describe a single experience when they felt a teacher had reached out with compassion and tenderness and tried to understand their feelings. They wanted someone to stop them from "being bad." Dr. LeShan concluded: "Some of our children may look tough and do dangerous things, but under the defenses against pain children are frightened and little, desperately wanting to be loved and understood and cared for." She said the way teachers and students reach each other is through shared feelings.

There was a letter to "Dear Abby" stating that the writer had no desire to return to a high school reunion. After all these years the hurt, the bitterness, the hostility that high school brought to mind were still there. Too many people feel this way. I feel we have a responsibility as educators to make schools safe, happy places for all students.

You cannot teach a man anything.
You can only help him discover it within himself.

—*Galileo*

7

CREATING A HUMANE ENVIRONMENT IN THE CLASSROOM

The whole art of teaching is only the art of awakening the natural curiosity of young minds . . . I know Jeanne! If that child were entrusted to my care, I should make of her . . . a child full of life, in whom everything beautiful in art and nature would awaken some gentle responsive thrill . . . I would make loveable to her everything I would wish her to love.

—Anatole France from *The Crime of Sylvestre Bonnard*

Creating a humane environment in the classroom is one of the greatest responsibilities of a teacher. Students do not naturally enter a classroom in the fall intending to love, like, and respect each other. Nor do they come intending to be disruptive and to create havoc in the classroom. They need a teacher to guide them into becoming productive, successful people in an atmosphere that brings out their very best, for their sake as well as the sake of their classmates. And you, as the teacher, want to live and work in such a place. But it takes work. Just as you teach cognitive skills, you must teach the children social skills—how to live and work with each other in a place that is safe for all physically, mentally, emotionally, and socially. This is done

through something called bonding. Teachers must intervene in things that are not emotionally good for children, i.e., putting each other down, making fun of each other, etc. You must have a plan to work on these problems just as you have a plan for teaching reading and math. *S.T.E.T.: Systematic Training for Effective Teaching,* and *The Encouragement Book,* by Don Dinkmeyer and Lewis E. Losoncy, are available to help you in this area. Another good source is *A Peaceable Classroom,* by Merril Harmin and Saville Sax.

A humane environment is reflected in a physically attractive classroom. It is one in which there is order. Materials are where they are supposed to be. There is a good management system, and the students know how to work successfully in this context. Beautiful posters, pictures, and students' work decorate the room. There is pride of ownership in the classroom, and students are empowered to take responsibility for their learning, free to take risks. Sometimes when they are doing artwork, lovely music may be playing in the background. The teacher is a learner along with the students. They know the teacher is not perfect. Once, when I had dressed hurriedly and appeared at school wearing two different shoes, I had my students' scrutiny to contend with. When they realized I was managing the situation well and was not dismayed by my error, they smiled as if to say, Hey, if the teacher can come to school wearing different shoes and not be upset, what can I do in life that's any worse than that? It was an accident, but I could not have planned a better lesson.

There should be a place for playfulness between teacher and students, between students and students. One April Fools' Day I filled the board with morning work, which I meant to erase as soon as I finished taking attendance. I was going to say, "April Fool!" The class grumbled. Then I had to leave the room for an urgent telephone call. When I returned, a child was stretched out on the floor, another child bent over him. She said, "Mrs. Hartline, he fell out of his seat, and I can't wake him up." There was total silence in the room. I ran and dropped to my knees over the child. Suddenly he let out a whoop, threw his arms around me, and the whole class yelled, "April Fool!" Obviously this was a frightening experience for me for the

moment, but when I recovered, I thought about their planning to play a joke on me. I thought it was rather creative. And we all had a good laugh together.

Let's look at bonding. From the first day of school the teacher should make a concerted effort to bring the students together like a family. There should be a format and a plan to solve problems. There should be activities planned that will allow the children to interact with each other socially and emotionally. The teacher should work to achieve a classroom climate where all students feel safe and valued as human beings. They may not all learn to love and like each other, but they can learn to respect each other and themselves. Teachers are the key to motivation. They have the huge responsibility of making each child feel worthwhile and successful. We can't teach children anything until we build good self-concepts.

In working on this theory, I have seen amazing things happen. Even as a beginning teacher, I felt deep within me the need to establish a rapport between a child and myself before trying to teach subject matter. And ever since, I have found it tremendously challenging to take a class, collectively and individually, and help them to believe in themselves.

When I was a classroom teacher, I always met my class outside the building before school. As they lined up to enter the building, we established an attitude toward school for the day. I tried to meet them with enthusiasm and a smile, as if to say, "Aren't we glad we're here? It's going to be a good day!" After all, a day at school might be the best thing that's going to happen to a child in a twenty-four-hour period.

The room was organized so that, once inside, the children earned the right to responsibilities and privileges. For example, I would say, "If you want to go to the library to do research or check out a book, just pick up the pass on the chalk rail by the door and go," indicating that they were entrusted to do so until or unless they abused the privilege.

During the day, I allowed for time to talk with my pupils—happy talk, sad talk, inconsequential talk—about things that mattered to them.

At the end of the day, I tried to send my pupils home happy and feeling that they had accomplished something, looking forward to tomorrow. I tried to leave them with an expectation for a special activity.

Once a fellow teacher heard me holding out especially challenging work as frosting on the cake. "You can't have this until you have finished your other work. Getting this work is a privilege." She called me a con artist, but she meant it as a compliment, and I took it that way. I thought, I should be a salesperson. I have a good product and the greatest customers in the world.

A humane environment is one that fosters academic success for all students. The teacher should be well prepared in the subject matter and offer group and individual lessons that will meet the needs of all the students. Then life should be breathed into these lessons. Enthusiasm and a love of learning are essential; students will follow your lead. The video *The Truth about Teachers* would be wonderful to share with faculties. It reminds us of why we went into teaching—to make it good for them, the students.

Being well prepared helps teachers stay on top of potential discipline problems. Having a plan for the day and sharing it with our students will put most of them on task, freeing us to work with those students who have problems with self-control. While the class can be enlisted to help with the more difficult students, the teacher must set the plan in motion. Here is an example of what I mean. The names of the children have been changed.

• • • • • • • • • • • • •

One year in my fourth-grade class there was a student with a multitude of problems. He visited every special-area teacher who was available. Once, as Jack left the room at the beginning of the day, I heard the students discussing where he went all day. They decided he probably went to the speech teacher. Or maybe to the learning disabilities teacher. They guessed every special teacher and said why they thought Jack probably had to go there. As I finished taking attendance and pulled my tall, red stool into the middle of the room, I said, "Let's talk about this. What are Jack's problems?" The children began listing things they had observed about this student, i.e., picks on big kids on the playground and gets beat up, blows on his arm and keeps it wet, red, and raw, does not do his work, tries to take the hamsters out of the cage, and on and on. Then I asked them what they thought we could do to help Jack. The hands flew. "We can let him eat lunch with us." "We can let him play with us on the playground and keep him away from the big kids who hurt him." "We can help him with his work." "We can let him play with the hamsters when he wants to and that will be okay with us."

When Jack returned, the plan went into operation. The first thing he did was to go the hamster cage. He took one out, and no one paid any attention to him. So far so good. He took it back to his desk; no one said anything. He let it run around on his desk for a few minutes, then he returned it to the cage. Brenda moved toward him and said, "Jack, let me help you with your spelling work." Jack didn't accomplish much spelling that day; he was just awed that beautiful Brenda, who attended the gifted program, was spending time helping him. I must point out that until this time he did not call me by name but touched me to get my attention. In his troubled little world he hardly recognized or knew the children by name. As they moved in to help him, they became names and people to him. He was made to feel included and a part of the class. One day we had to leave the room quickly for a fire drill. Jack, who had taken a hamster to his seat, stuffed the fuzzy critter inside the desk as he left. When we returned, he discovered that the hamster had devoured a corner of his apparently edible spelling book. Everyone gathered around and had a good laugh. I never will forget Jack's face as he looked around at the other students as they shared this funny moment with him. Spelling books can be replaced, but children can't. The warmth of that moment was very special.

We went on a field trip and lost Jack three times, and they found him each time. They gently took his arm down when he nervously started blowing on it. They protected him on the playground by including him in their activities. I watched this child as he slowly began to trust the children and learned to relate to them. We all learned a lot from Jack about caring and understanding.

• • • • • • • • • • • •

And then there was Jamie. He came after school had started. As the saying goes, he was something else! He came with a history of discipline problems. Again, the students rallied around him and helped him assimilate into the class. It was a struggle for awhile, but then I began to notice that Jamie was showing great improvement. I asked him to stay after school one afternoon while I wrote a note home. I noticed he was breathing very heavily while I wrote. When I finished I read the note to him. It said he was doing much better in school and that I was very proud of him. He literally grabbed the note and ran home. The next morning he came to me and said, "My mother said we are going to keep that note forever. They ain't never said anything good about me at school before." At the end of the year he asked if he could sit on my tall, red stool and speak to the class. He thanked them for helping him, and said he had not done anything for them. Oh, yes, you did, Jamie. You taught us patience and tolerance!

• • • • • • • • • • • •

An activity I used at the beginning of the year to help my students get to know each other was one called Secret Friends.

On Monday I put their names on folded pieces of paper in a box. I told them they were going to draw a name, and that person would be their secret friend for a week. After they looked at the name they had drawn, I collected the pieces of paper and destroyed them. They were to tell no one whose name they had! Then they were to do nice things for that person all week. I told them to be nice to several people so it would be harder to guess who their secret friend was. On Friday they guessed who they thought their secret friend was, and why. They had great fun guessing, and learning whether they had been right. This activity helped them to learn the names of their classmates and to get to know each other.

Teachers can share themselves with children. The students need to know that, yes, the teacher is really a human being. Yes, I have a family. Yes, I hurt just as you do. Yes, I am very happy today. Would you like to know why?

Once I read that a child thought teachers lived in the teachers' lounge and emerged each morning. Whose fault is this?

Teachers can tell personal stories to children. This was one of my favorite stories to share with a class where there were children with reading problems.

One night when my daughter was just learning to read, she and her dad were sitting on the couch. His arm was around her, and she was reading away.

Passing through the room, I stopped and said, "Just listen to her. Isn't that great! Aren't you proud of her?"

He looked at me and said, "Why, I was proud of her when she couldn't read one word!"

As I finished this story, my children looked relieved. Their faces seemed to say, Okay, so I've got a reading problem, but no big deal. I can be liked and loved for just being me.

On sharing with students, Albert Cullum in *The Geranium on the Window Sill Just Died But Teacher You Went Right On,* says, "On the morning you tell us about the night before, you're like one of us. The dress you bought, or a movie you saw, or a strange sound you heard. You're a good storyteller, teacher, honest! And that's when I never have to be excused."

One of the best ways to bond a class together is to read to them. I read to my students every day after lunch. I firmly believe this quote from Glenna Davis Sloan from *The Child as a Critic:* "Literacy begins in hearts not heads. There is a story or poem to raise a goose bump on the toughest skin, and we are well advised to find it. A child never thrilled to words will remain indifferent to reading or writing them."

I chose books they could not read for themselves. I read *Jonathan Livingston Seagull,* by Richard Bach, to my fourth-graders. They were enthralled with the story. When I read the part where Jonathan was flying way up high where seagulls were not supposed to be able to fly, Guy said softly, "Why, the little devil!" No one laughed. Everyone was

soaring with Jonathan. Stacey wrote Richard Bach to tell him how much we enjoyed the book, and he wrote back on seagull paper, "I'm glad you liked Jonathan."

When reading *The Little Prince,* by Antoine de Saint-Exupéry, we discussed the dialogue between the Little Prince and the fox, which they illustrated and included in their *ME!?* books. In this dialogue the fox tells the Little Prince that though they are parting, the lovely things he sees around him would always remind him of their newfound friendship. As a parallel, I told my students that we would spend one year together and then go our separate ways, but we would always be a part of each other for the special time we had spent together. I told them to remember always that there was once a teacher who believed in them, and they were never to forget it, no matter what happened to them in life. And I have received letters from some who said they did remember later when life got tough, and that it did help.

A wonderful book I used for teaching children not to make fun of each other is *The Hundred Dresses,* by Eleanor Estes. This is a safe way to teach such lessons. The problem is Wanda's in the book, and the children can safely discuss her problem and solutions to such a problem. At the end of the Children's Bibliography in this book I have listed some good resources for finding books that deal with bibliotherapy.

I shared a very special book with my students entitled *Hope for the Flowers,* by Trina Paulus. It's a book that takes about forty-five minutes to read to a class. The story of Stripe and Yellow is a spellbinder. Why be a fuzzy worm when potentially you are a beautiful butterfly? It is not about caterpillars and butterflies. Rather it is about people becoming the best they can be.

Teacher expectation is very important when looking at a class collectively and individually. You usually get what you expect! I always tried to make it a point not to look at the cumulative records of my students at the beginning of the year or listen to the horror stories in the teachers' lounge. I didn't want to get preconceived ideas about them academically or socially. One year, during the first week of school, we went to the library, and I asked for a library helper. for the first period of school. All hands went up. One little boy looked at me with such pleading blue eyes, I chose him. What an outburst! Every child started saying what a bad boy Bill had been in third grade. Even the librarian looked at me rather strangely. Through all of this the child held his head high, even though his chin was quivering. He watched me, and I looked straight into his eyes and said, "I think I have chosen the right person." He never let me down. I never knew the Bill who was so notorious.

We need to have high expectations

for our students, set them up for success, and then praise them. I always told them to be on their best behavior when there was a substitute in the room. One year I had a student who had a lot of trouble with self-control. I pulled him aside one day and said, "Jim, I love you very much, but I certainly don't like your behavior right now." One day when he was disrupting the class, I stood up quickly and said his name. He said, "I know, Mrs. Hartline, you love me, you just don't like what I am doing right now." "Exactly," I said. "Cut it out." The lesson here is to separate the child from the deed. When I knew I was going to be away, I put Jim in charge of the substitute, so he would not wipe her out! Invariably, when I would return, there would be a note from the substitute saying what a wonderful class they were. Then she would say that one child in particular was especially helpful—Jim. The children loved to hear these good reports, and I always told them the nice things that were said about them. They worked hard to live up to their good reputation.

Let me share with you the apocryphal story of a teacher in an inner-city school. On the first day of the school year, she quickly picked up the materials in her box and hurried to her classroom. Around Christmas time, the principal thought he had better check on her, because he knew she had a "difficult" class. He entered a room filled with happy, busy children, and he watched in amazement. Finally, he whispered to her, "My God, what's going on? Didn't you see their IQ scores?" She looked puzzled for a moment and then said, "Oh, I thought those were their locker numbers." This teacher *believed* in her students.

It takes a lot of work on a teacher's part to bond a class together, but the rewards are great. I like to think that when we get it all pulled together, it feels like this as described by George B. Leonard in *Education and Ecstasy:* "How many of those times do you remember? SOMETHING HAPPENS. A delicate warmth slides into parts of your being you did not even realize were cold. The marrow of your bones begins to thaw. You feel a little lurch as your own consciousness, the teacher's voice, the entire web of sound and silence that hold the class together, the room itself, the very flow of time all shift to a different level. And suddenly it is Christmas morning, with students and teacher exchanging delightful gifts while bells silently chime; the old furniture around the room reflects a holiday gleam; your classmates' eyes sparkle and snap like confetti and you realize with the certainty of music how rare and valuable each inhabitant of that room has become, has always been. Or you find yourself trembling slightly with the terror and joy of knowledge, the immensity of existence and pattern and change. And when it ends and you must leave, you reel from the room with flushed face, knowing you will never again be quite the same. You have learned."

"He drew a circle that shut me out—heretic, rebel, a thing to flout,
but love and I had the wit to win. We drew a circle that took him in."

—Edwin Markham

8

METHOD OF TEACHING
SELF-ESTEEM IN THE CLASSROOM

Interest Center

INTRODUCTORY LESSONS

For the study of self in the classroom, an "interest center" is an excellent focal point. (Please note the diagram that accompanies the pictures of the interest center. The first list indicates the part that books play in this study—books for the teacher's personal growth, resource books for the teacher to draw upon for activities, books to read to the students, books for students to read, and books to share with parents. The second list is for films that are to be used, each one correlated with a particular lesson, i.e., "Crossbar" could be used when an activity in goal-setting is used. The third list defines activities that can be brought into the study, i.e., the I.A.L.A.C. story, the process of Magic Circle, journal writing, etc.)

I will now tell you how the study of self was introduced in the classroom. My experience in working with teachers has taught me that their creativity takes over once they have seen this model. They create their own centers, drawing from

their own personal philosophies, their resources, their ideas, their favorite things, and their talents. The sky's the limit when you get started!

Prepare a Bulletin Board

There are several commercial bulletin boards on self-esteem that you may purchase. Or you can create your own bulletin board. This board will stay up all year as the backdrop for your center. Laminating the bulletin board will help to preserve it. I also like to put a mirror in the center of it, so children can look into it and see themselves.

Prepare an Interest Center and Set Up in Classroom

Look at the picture of the interest center. In front of the bulletin board on the left-hand side is a box entitled "Teacher's Resources." This is your retrieval box for collecting activities, poems, songs, stories, etc., for your particular grade level. The box to the right is the file for storing the students' books about themselves. (If they keep them at their desk, they may lose them, misplace loose sheets, etc.) We talk about trust—that no one will look at their book unless they choose to share. The box in the middle is where activity sheets are kept for students to use in compiling their Me Books. There are many resources for these activity books, which you will find in the resource section of this book. I have also provided some activity sheets to get you started. Some of the teachers in my classes are now creating their own activity sheets. Some teachers are naturally artistic, and some are using their computers to design the sheets. And there are always artistic students whose talents you can draw upon.

When the bulletin board is completed and you have set up the interest center, plan a time to introduce it. Discuss with your students that this is a different kind of interest center, whose subject will be the student. Through written and oral activities, group discussions, books, films, kits, and other materials, they will be learning about themselves. Tell the students how long you plan to have the center, i.e., six weeks, a semester, or a whole year. Discuss some of the things they think they might be learning and why you feel it is important to have this interest center. Discuss some probable outcomes of such a study and the impact it could have on the class individually and collectively. This would be a good time to discuss the meaning of self-concept, self-esteem, and why one's self-esteem is important.

LESSON #1: Design a Cover

Materials needed: Construction paper or commercial folders with pockets inside, Magic Markers, crayons, pencils.

Tell the students that they are going to be writing a book about themselves. Brainstorm some ideas for titles. Write some of the suggestions on the board. The teacher might show the class some examples of covers she has made. Explain that the students will be the authors of their own books and are to design the covers the way they want them. Construction paper/folders should be kept in the interest center in case some students want to make new covers as the unit progresses. Completed covers can be filed in the interest center's student retrieval box.

LESSON #2: Write a Paragraph

Materials needed: The *Greatest Salesman in the World* by Og Mandino, the sheets "I like being me because . . ." (from this chapter), ink pads, pencils.

Read or paraphrase from *The Greatest Salesman in the World* "I Am Nature's Greatest Miracle." Here you could substitute one of your favorite books or pieces that illustrates individual uniqueness. *The Important Book* by Margaret Wise Brown would be a good one for primary children. Discuss with the class their individuality, that they are "one of a kind." Discuss ways in which we are the same, i.e., basic needs of food, water, shelter, etc., and ways we are different, i.e., physical appearances, families, tastes in food, clothing, interests, etc. Discuss that we all have a need to be loved, to belong to a family, to have a sense of security, and to have ways to express ourselves as worthwhile human beings.

Discuss that the class will be writing a paragraph entitled "I like being me because . . ." The teacher can role play with a student in front of the class with first the teacher and then the student saying, "I like being me because . . ." Other students may want to volunteer and participate. This will give them ideas for writing their paragraphs.

While the students are writing their paragraphs, the teacher might start a "Me" vocabulary list, employing words the students will use as they are writing their paragraphs, i.e., friend, mother, father, brother, sister, love, God, etc. The words could be put on a chart, and other words added as the unit develops.

While the students are writing their paragraphs, the teacher can go around with an ink pad and let each student put their thumbprint at the top of the page. Discuss the uniqueness of thumbprints and how everyone's is different, even identical twins'. Over the years I have done this many times with hundreds of students, and have learned to use a self-fulfilling prophecy concept: As I hold the student's hand I say to myself, May this student never be fingerprinted except for good things in life.

The students, if they wish, may share their paragraphs when they are completed. No one should ever be forced to share any of their activities. This will be the first page in their book unless you have chosen to use a title page. Tell the students that blank "I like being me because . . ." sheets will be available in the interest center, if they want to write

another one at another time. It takes awhile to think positively about one's self.

LESSON #3: Thumbprint Art
Materials needed: *Great Thumbprint Drawing Book,* by Ed Emberley, thumbprint sheet provided in this chapter, ink pads in different colors, pencils, crayons.

This is a continuation of Lesson #2. Go back and discuss what we learned about all fingerprints being different, even identical twins'. Discuss what this tells us about ourselves. Show the pictures in the *Great Thumbprint Drawing Book.* Use the picture of the flowers and tell the students that, if everyone did a flower picture, they would all be different, because their thumbprints are different. Let students do their thumbprint art, then display them on a bulletin board entitled, "I'm Thumbody Special!" This sheet will later go into their books.

LESSON #4: "I Am" Wheel Activity (provided in this chapter)
Materials needed: "I Am" wheels, pencils, colored pencils or crayons.

Give each student a copy of this activity. Go over the directions. The teacher can read the survey or have students do it alone. Provide time for students to color their wheels. After the wheels are completed, discuss individual differences. These wheels might be displayed on a bulletin board. Suggest the students do another wheel at the end of the unit so they can see how they change as they grow and learn. This activity will also go into their books.

LESSON #5: *ME!?* Collage
Materials needed: Tagboard, old magazines, scissors, paste. The teacher could use the silhouettes provided in this chapter and then mount them on construction paper, cut around the silhouette, and have a frame for the collage.

Tell the students they are to look through the magazines and find pictures and words that describe themselves. This is a particularly good activity for encouraging students to talk with each other, share their thoughts and feelings about their likes and dislikes, interests, etc. This activity will take more than one period of time. After the collages are completed, they may share them, if they wish to, by discussing them or by displaying them on a bulletin board. Some students may want to frame them and hang them in their rooms at home.

LESSON #6: Begin Activity Sheets
Materials needed: Activity sheets from many books or activity sheets provided in chapter nine, pencils, crayons.

It is not necessary for the teacher to have all the sheets ready at this time. Some can be run off each week and added to the middle box in the center. Start the students together, but later let them make choices of the sheets they wish to complete. They may color the artwork on the activity sheets to make them more attractive. These sheets will comprise the bulk of their *ME!?* books.

When will your students work on their *ME!?* books? This will be up to you. I had designated times when my classes worked on the books. I had other interest centers in the classroom, so sometimes the *ME!?* Center was one of the choices when they had completed their basic work. There were times when they settled in with their *ME!?* books when I was reading to them after lunch. Yes, they can listen, write, and color all at the same time!

Other things can be added to their *ME!?* books: poems like "Thumbprint," and "Me, Myself, and I," by Eve Merriam, and "Me," by Walter de la Mare. Some of my students illustrated their poems. Some wrote their own poems, and shared them and put them in their *ME!?* books.

When I read a favorite book like *The Velveteen Rabbit,* by Margery Williams, the children illustrated the passage from the book entitled "What Is Real?" and included this in their books. The dialogue between the Little Prince and the fox from *The Little Prince,* by Antoine de Saint-Exupéry, is another favorite which they illustrated and included in their *ME!?* books. Quotes and favorite sayings were also illustrated and included. Sometimes a student created something and wanted it reproduced for everyone in the class. Sometimes they just added personal things they wanted to include in their own books. The books truly became special to them, and some of my students who are now adults tell me they still have their *ME!?* books. These books serve an important function in the development of self-awareness.

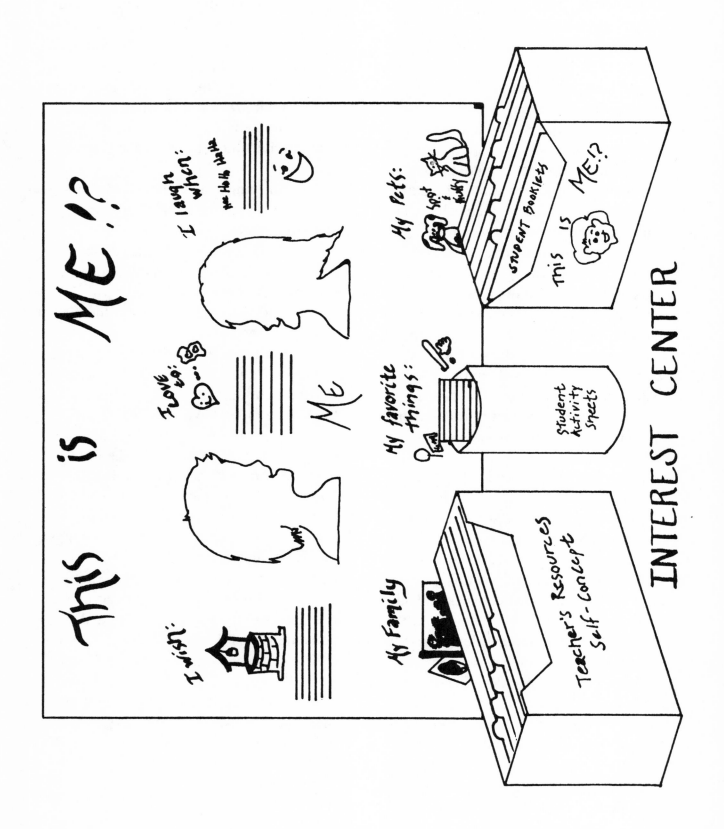

BOOKS

For teacher for own awareness:
Born to Win, Jongeward and James
Love, Buscaglia
Teacher Effectiveness Training, Gordon
Celebrate the Self, Briggs

For teacher for ideas for activities:
100 Ways to Enhance Self-Concept in the Classroom, Wells and Canfield
Self-Esteem: A Classroom Affair, vols. 1 & 2, Borba
Esteem Builders, Borba

For teacher to read to students:
Bells of Freedom, Butters
Charlotte's Web, White
Hope for the Flowers, Paulus
The Little Prince, Saint-Exupéry
Skeezer: The Dog with a Mission, Yates
The Velveteen Rabbit, Williams

For students to read:
Girl of Limberlost, Porter
The Hundred Dresses, Estes
Swimmy, Lionni
A Tiger Called Thomas, Zolotow

For parents to read:
For the Love of Children, Ford
Parent Effectiveness Training, Gordon
Your Child's Self-Esteem, Briggs

Films

Angel and Big Joe
Cipher in the Snow
A Desk for Billie
A Different Kind of Winning
The Emmet Smith Story
Family of Strangers
Feeling Left Out
The Hundred Penny Box
I'm Somebody Special
Johnny Baker's Last Race
Johnny Lingo
Mandy's Grandmother
Nobody's Useless
Shopping Bag Lady
Sunshine's on the Way
Take a Look at Yourself
The Tap Dance Kid
There's Nobody Else Like You
They Call Me Names
The Ugly Little Boy
Uncle Ben
Very Special Friends
What About Thad?

OTHER ACTIVITIES

Bulletin Boards
Eye Can/I Can
Games
"I Am" Wheel
Journal Writing
Kits (T.A., Duso)
Literature
Magic Circle
Music
Poetry
Poor Worm
Posters

I LIKE BEING ME

because _____

_____

_____

_____

_____

_____

_____

_____

_____

_____

_____

_____

_____

_____

My
Thumbprint Artwork

Here is a copy of <u>MY</u> Thumb Print.

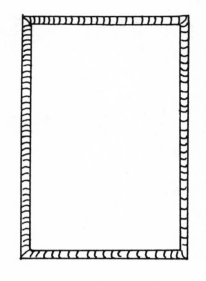

Since I am unique and
special in all the World,
I plan to make a difference in the World by

_____

_____

_____

_____

_____

_____

_____

_____

_____

_____

THE "I AM" WHEEL GAME

The "I Am" wheel is a game which helps each person to illustrate likes and dislikes and the things he or she is good at or not so good at.

On the line following each item _____
Write the number 1 if the item is something in which you have a very high interest.
Write the number 2 if the item is something in which you have an average interest.
Write the number 3 if the item is something in which your interest is low.
Write the number 4 if the item is something in which you have no interest whatsoever.

1. food _____
2. airplanes _____
3. history _____
4. having friends _____
5. school _____
6. opera _____
7. meeting new people _____
8. science _____
9. ecology _____
10. haunted houses _____
11. poetry _____
12. stage plays _____
13. going to parties _____
14. flowers _____
15. mythology _____
16. astronomy _____
17. television _____
18. travel _____
19. guns _____
20. making good grades _____
21. costumes _____
22. ESP _____
23. rocks _____
24. playing records _____
25. pets _____
26. summer _____
27. winter _____
28. fall _____
29. spring _____
30. summer _____
31. having new clothes _____
32. ballet _____
33. hiking _____
34. dinosaurs _____
35. books
36. gardening _____
37. helping at home _____
38. animals _____

39. games _____

40. pop music _____

41. warfare _____

42. music _____

43. making money _____

44. photography _____

45. being a good citizen _____

46. learning new things _____

47. classical music _____

48. concerts _____

49. dolls _____

50. conversation _____

51. movies _____

52. radio disk jockeys _____

53. politics _____

54. arithmetic _____

55. religion _____

56. cars _____

57. space travel _____

58. art _____

59. sports _____

60. architecture _____

61. health _____

62. geography _____

On the line following each item_____
Write the number 1 if the item is something you do very well.
Write the number 2 if the item is something you do with average skill.
Write the number 3 if the item is something you do poorly.
Write the number 4 if the item is something you cannot do.

63. wrestling _____

64. ice skating _____

65. saw boards _____

66. skiing _____

67. doing cartwheels _____

68. arithmetic _____

69. thinking _____

70. talking _____

71. building models _____

72. roller skating _____

73. singing _____

74. turning somersaults _____

75. using a camera _____

76. playing chess _____

77. throwing a softball _____

78. riding a bicycle _____

79. shot putting _____

80. making up poems _____

81. acting _____

82. taking care of pets _____

83. running _____

84. playing golf _____

85. writing _____

86. high jumping _____

87. yo-yoing _____

88. making things _____

89. solving problems _____

90. hitting a ball _____

91. playing hopscotch _____
92. broad jumping _____
93. throwing a Frisbee _____
94. telling jokes _____
95. following directions _____
96. playing marbles _____
97. pole vaulting _____
98. playing a musical instrument

_____
99. imitating _____
100. playing basketball _____
101. drawing _____
102. dancing _____
103. rope climbing _____
104. planting flowers _____
105. cooking _____
106. throwing a football _____
107. reading _____
108. playing jacks _____
109. repairing things _____
110. playing checkers _____
111. playing softball _____
112. making speeches _____
113. speaking in a foreign language

_____

114. sewing _____
115. playing volleyball _____
116. diving _____
117. selling things _____
118. solving puzzles _____
119. playing tennis _____
120. fishing _____
121. spelling _____
122. skipping rope _____
123. drawing maps _____
124. playing card games _____
125. hunting _____
126. trapshooting _____
127. digging holes _____
128. being a leader _____
129. chopping wood _____
130. using a map _____
131. observing _____
132. swimming _____
133. hammering nails _____
134. listening _____
135. planting vegetables _____
136. giving first aid _____

INSTRUCTIONS

On the circle graph, find the number that corresponds with each number on your survey sheet. Be as neat as possible. Color the numbered segment on the circle graph as follows:

Red ....if your answer was 1   Blue ....if your answer was 3
Green ......if your answer was 2   Orange ....if your answer was 4
If you are a boy ......color ring A green   If you are a girl ......color ring A blue
In ring B, draw and color vivid images from a recent dream or nightmare.
Make ring C your favorite color.

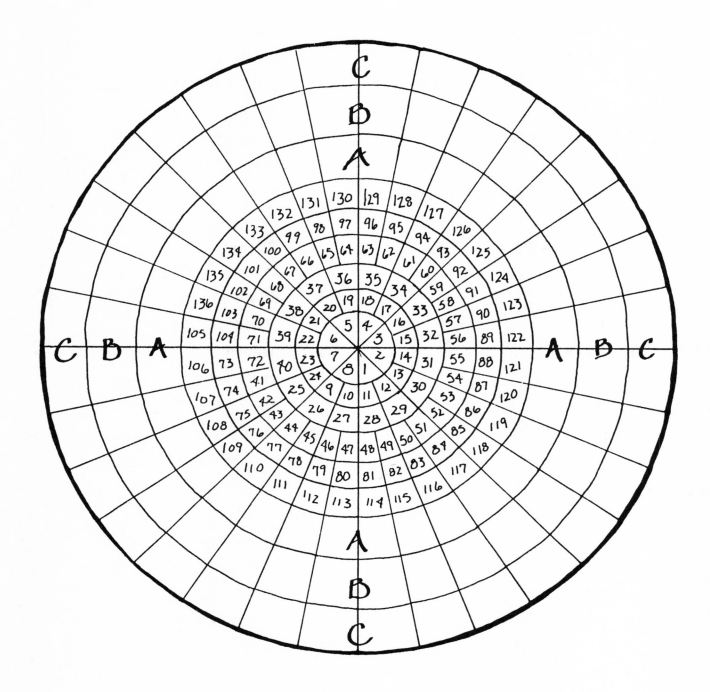

"I AM" WHEEL

"I Am" Wheel

ACTIVITY

Give a set of the "I Am" materials to each pupil and ask him or her to complete it.

EVALUATION

Display the "I Am" wheels for a few days so that each child can come to appreciate the individual differences. The awareness that differences are "normal" should bring evidence of increased tolerance among the children.

MATERIALS NEEDED

Per student: copy of interest-ability survey and circle graph with coloring instructions, crayons.

SUGGESTED FOLLOW-UP

1. Retain the student's wheel in his or her folder and have him or her do a second wheel late in the year to illustrate the change.
2. The "I Am" wheels will make a colorful, interesting display for open house.
3. The "I Am" wheel would make an appropriate illustration for the cover of a diary.
4. A student's wheel from one year might be compared to his or her wheel in the following year to illustrate changes.

Used with permission
Arizona State Department of Education
Phoenix, Arizona

48   ME!?

9

ME!? BOOK
ACTIVITY SHEETS

My Very Special Book about

ME

Write several sentences on each topic. Write about your feelings and facts of the topic. Color the pictures and create your own.

I'm Glad , I'm ME!

No one looks
The way I do.
I have noticed
That it's true:
   No one walks
   The Way I walk.
   No one talks
   The way I talk.
   No one plays
   The way I play.
   No one Says
   The things I Say.
I'm Special
I AM ME!
There's no one
I would rather be!

—Author Unknown

My Vital Statistics

I am _____ years old.

I have _____ eyes and _____ hair.

I am ____'____" tall.

You would recognize me because I am

_____

_____

_____

_____

_____

_____

_____

Name: _____

Date: _____

I Like
Being ME
Because

_____
_____
_____
_____
_____
_____
_____
_____
_____
_____
_____

I make
a good friend
because

_____
_____
_____
_____
_____
_____
_____

My Birthday is a Special time for ME.

This is a Birthday I remember. _____
_____
_____
_____
_____
_____
_____
_____

Friends
are
important
in my life.
To ME
a
friend is

_____

_____

_____

_____

_____

_____

_____

_____

_____

_____

_____

Each Holiday has
Special meaning but
my favorite holiday is
_____

I remember once on
this holiday
_____
_____
_____
_____
_____
_____
_____
_____
_____
_____

Jan.
Feb.
Sweetheart
Mar.
April
Fool
May
June
Dad
July
Aug.
Vacation
Time
Sept.
Oct.
Nov.
Dec.
Ho Ho

In the timeline of
my life the event
that stands out the
most is _____

_____

_____

_____

_____

_____

_____

_____

_____

_____

_____

12

9   3

6

1
yr.

6
yr.

5
yr.

4
yr.

3
yr.   2 yr   1 yr

My Mother and Father
have told ME Stories about
When I was a little kid.
Here is one of the Stories
I like best. _____
_____
_____
_____
_____
_____
_____
_____
_____

HA HA HA HA HA HA HA HA HA HA HA HA HA HA HA HA HA

HA

HA

HA

HA

HA

HA

HA

HA

HA

HA

HA

HA

HA

HA

HA

HA

HA

Having a sense of humor is a special gift in life. Something that tickles my funnybone is

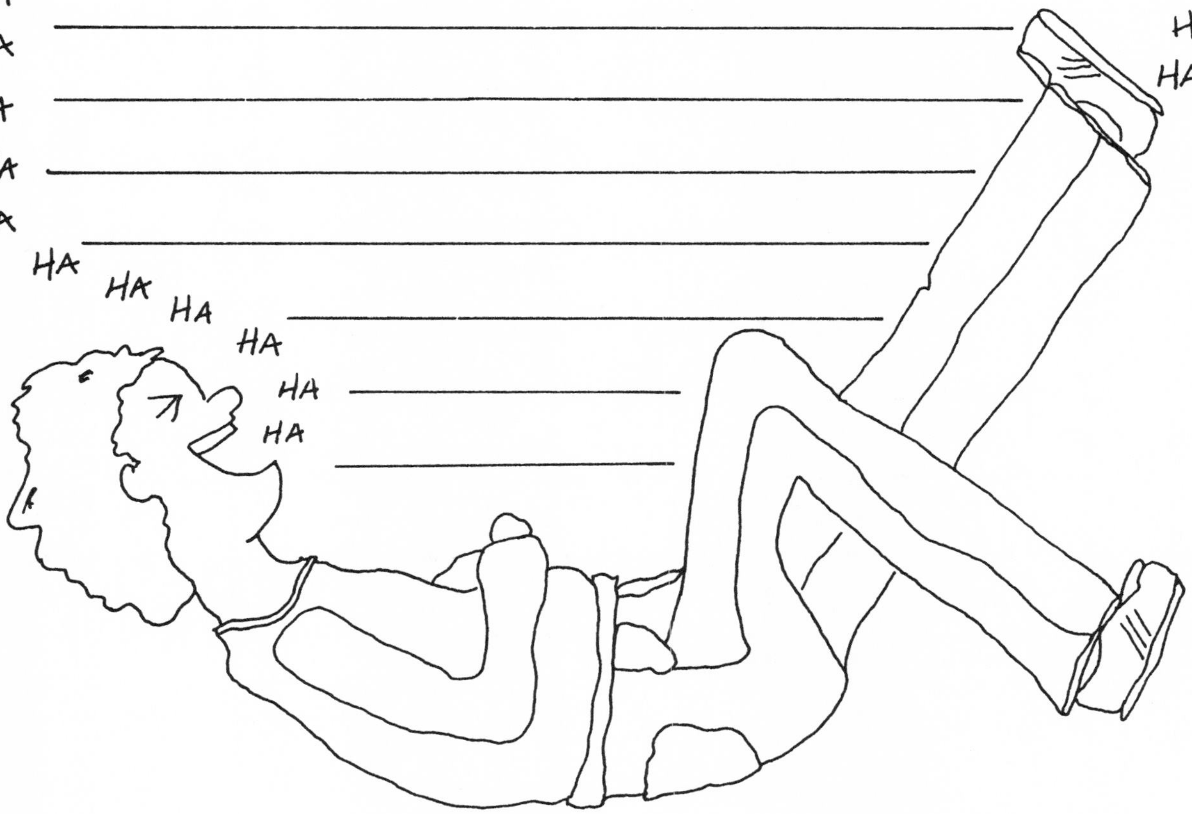

_____

_____

_____

_____

_____

_____

_____

_____

_____

_____

HA   HA   HA

HA

HA

HA

If I could make an outstanding contribution to the World,

I would

_____

_____

_____

_____

_____

_____

_____

_____

_____

_____

_____

It is not always easy being a kid. This is one of my greatest worries and my way of dealing with it. _____

_____

_____

_____

_____

_____

_____

_____

_____

_____

12

My favorite time of day
is _____. I like it
because _____

_____
_____
_____
_____

9

3

_____
_____
_____
_____

6

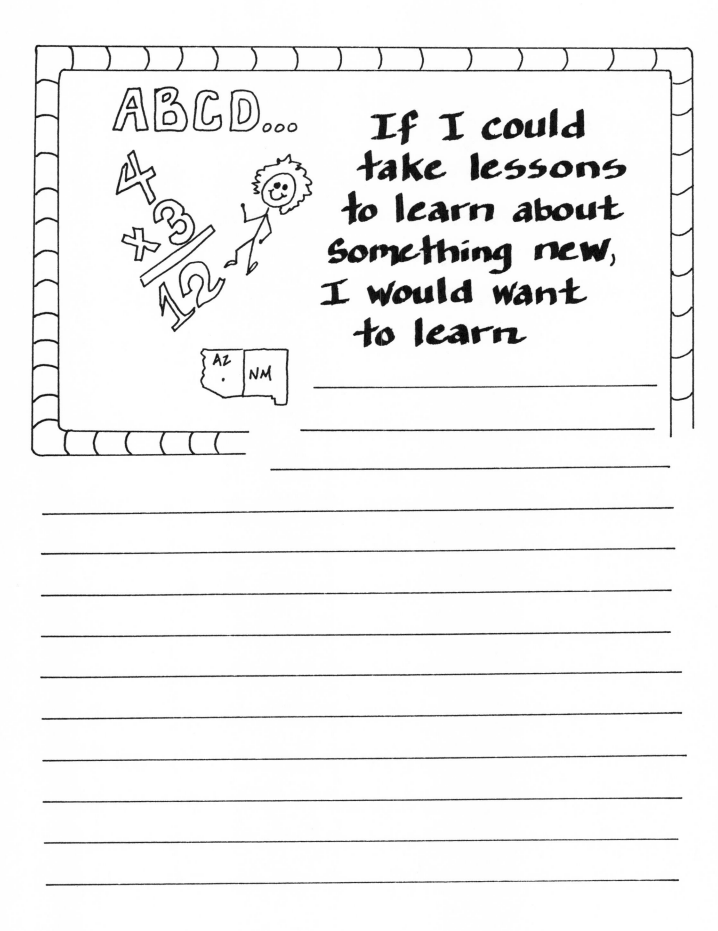

ABCD...

4 ×3/12

AZ · NM

If I could take lessons to learn about something new, I would want to learn

My pet is an
important part of my
life. Here is a story
about my pet and ME.

_____
_____
_____
_____
_____
_____
_____
_____
_____
_____
_____

This is the name of
a person who makes
ME feel like an
important person:
_____

This person makes
ME feel important because

_____

_____

_____

_____

_____

_____

_____

_____

_____

_____

_____

When I was a little kid I had a favorite toy. This is the name of the toy and why it was special to ME.

Wishes can become Goals for Life.
One of my biggest wishes is

_____

_____

_____

_____

_____

_____

_____

_____

_____

_____

_____

_____

If I went on a trip and could take only one possession I would take

_____

_____

_____

_____

_____

_____

_____

_____

_____

_____

_____

_____

If I could change places With Someone I would like to be _____

_____

_____

_____

_____

_____

My Family

plays a very important part in my
life. My family is special because

_____

_____

_____

_____

_____

_____

_____

_____

_____

_____

If I could plan my perfect Vacation, it would be

_____

_____

_____

_____

_____

_____

_____

_____

_____

_____

England —
Virgin Islands
See the USA
Mexico
Switerland —

VACATION LAND

Ski Vacation —

Sometimes
I
get
Angry!

These are
some
of the
things
that make
ME
mad.

_____
_____
_____
_____
_____
_____
_____
_____
_____
_____

There are times When I like to be alone.
One of these times is When

If I should ever write a song, it would be greatly influenced by this song or composer.

_____

_____

_____

_____

_____

_____

_____

_____

_____

I am an important member of my family because

_____

_____

_____

_____

_____

_____

_____

_____

These are the things that I like to do with my family.

_____

_____

_____

_____

_____

_____

_____

_____

_____

_____

If I could leave one thing to a grandchild, I would leave _____

_____

_____

_____

_____

_____

_____

_____

_____

_____

_____

_____

_____

As I look at Special times in my life, this was one of my happiest moments and Why it made me happy.

One of the best books I ever read was _____
This is why I liked it. _____
_____
_____
_____
_____
_____
_____
_____
_____

Everyone has strength and weakness. Something I am very good at doing is

_____

_____

_____

_____

_____

_____

_____

_____

_____

_____

_____

_____

_____

_____

There are times when I like to be with others. One of these times is _____

_____

_____

_____

_____

_____

_____

_____

_____

_____

_____

When I grow up I want to make a living by _____

_____

_____

_____

_____

_____

_____

_____

_____

_____

_____

_____

_____

_____

This is a book all about ME!? And this is how I would like to end my book.

(NAME of STUDENT)

has successfully
completed all
of the activities
of the "ME" unit!

(signature of teacher)

10
ACTIVITIES

One of my favorite activities is the I.A.L.A.C. story by Dr. Sidney Simon. I explain to the students that I.A.L.A.C. means I am lovable and capable if those who are significant in my life treat me that way. I have an I.A.L.A.C. sign already prepared as I start this lesson. This sign represents how we feel about ourselves. It is affected by how others treat us. If someone teases us, rejects us, or puts us down, then a piece of our I.A.L.A.C. sign is destroyed. I tear a piece of my sign to illustrate. Then I proceed to tell a story to illustrate a day in the life of an I.A.L.A.C. sign. (You may use the original story by Dr. Simon, make up one of your own at your grade level, or use the story that follows.) I tear the sign as I tell the story.

• • • • • • • • • • • •

One morning Susan was dressing for school. Her sister said, "You aren't going to wear that dress, are you? It looks terrible on you." (rip) She gets to the kitchen and her mother yells, "Susan, take out the garbage you forgot last night. You

never remember to do your chores." (rip) As she walks to school, someone pushes her off the sidewalk and says, "Get out of my way, Four-eyes," knocking her glasses to the pavement. (rip) Susan finally settles into her classroom at school. The spelling papers are handed back, and she has made an F. (rip) In the reading group she is passed over to read aloud even though she raises her hand to read. The teacher says, "Susan, you read too slowly." (rip) At recess Susan runs to join a game of four-square ball. The children push her aside and tell her they do not want her to play with them. (rip) In the lunchroom her best friend, Lindsay, has asked another girl to join her for lunch and ignores Susan. (rip) Susan walks home from school all alone, feeling that she has no friends. (rip) When she gets home no one is there, and her mother has forgotten to buy the after-school snack food. (rip) After dinner she asks her father to help her with her homework. He replies that he is too busy with his own work he brought home from the office. (rip) She decides to help her mother with the baby, but her mother pushes her aside and says that she is only getting in the way. (rip) Finally, when Susan decides to go to bed, she slowly takes off what is left of her I.A.L.A.C. sign.

• • • • • • • • • • • • •

After the story the class and I discuss what happened to Susan's I.A.L.A.C. sign during the course of the day. We discuss how our own I.A.L.A.C. signs can be torn and how we tear the signs of others. We discuss how we feel when our signs get torn and how we feel when we rip someone else's sign. We also discuss how our signs could be enlarged and how we could enlarge the sign of others.

At this point I explain to the students that people who have their signs all ripped up want to rip up the signs of others because they feel so bad. I ask them to try to remember this and not react to this hostility with their own hostility.

Sometimes our signs get ripped and the hurt is just hanging there. When this happens we can just look at the person and say, or say to ourselves, "No matter what you say about me, I am still a worthwhile human being." Sometimes I have them write this on the back of their I.A.L.A.C. sign. (I learned this technique in a seminar with Jack Canfield.)

Sometimes after I have done this activity in class with my students, I pin an I.A.L.A.C. sign on them to wear home. I tell them not to tell anyone what it means. They are to tear a piece of the sign if bad things happen to them, and put a smiley face on the sign if good things happen. The next day they are to tell me the story of their sign. That night I send home an explanation of the I.A.L.A.C. sign and a copy of "Did You Hug Your Child Today?" by Arlene Silberman.

With parents and teachers I do a similar version. I read the story, tearing the sign as I read. I also like to use the films *Cipher in the Snow* and *Johnny Lingo.* I read or paraphrase "Did You Hug Your Child Today?" We have a follow-up discussion on ways parents and teachers can enhance the self-esteem of their children.

One year when I did the I.A.L.A.C. story, one of my lively little boys came in the next morning without his sign. As he glanced around at everyone's sign, he asked, "Was I supposed to bring the pin back? They got my whole sign!" I said, "Jake, tell me what happened." "Well," he said, "when I walked in the door, my mother asked, 'What has that teacher pinned on you now?'" As a piece of paper fluttered to the floor, the mother said, "Look, dummy, you are messing up the house." Things went from bad to worse until the sign was all gone. Jake thoughtfully listened to all the stories of the other students. At the end of the day, when the others were gone, he approached me and said, "Hey, if you'll give me three of those signs, I'll make it through the weekend!" I hugged him and said, "Jake, that's what it is all about. You don't give up, and you are lovable and capable."

(The following is the explanation of the I.A.L.A.C. story I send to parents.)

I.A.L.A.C.

This is a story of a sign. It means I AM LOVABLE AND CAPABLE if those who are significant in my life treat me that way. To feel LOVABLE, I need you to say that I am lovable in as many ways as possible every day. I need to believe it! I need to feel good about me. I need to feel important to others.

I also need to feel CAPABLE. I need to feel that I can accomplish things . . . that I am a productive, worthwhile human being. I need opportunities to validate this.

I need you to help take care of my sign. I feel less lovable and capable when it gets ripped by thoughtless words and deeds. When mine gets ripped I may try to rip your sign to feel better. But this really doesn't work. We all need to take care of each other's signs. Remember, WE ARE ALL LOVABLE AND CAPABLE.

DID YOU HUG YOUR CHILD TODAY?
by Arlene Silberman

It was a perfect spring day. Clusters of honeysuckle sweetened the air and a profusion of lilacs lightened my heart as I drove along a wide, tree-shaded boulevard. Then, suddenly, a bumper sticker on the car directly ahead blasted my serenity. DID YOU HUG YOUR CHILD TODAY? the bold red letters challenged. I changed lanes. Minutes later, the bumper sticker reappeared, insisting that I face the question.

I shivered as I recalled the rat-a-tat-tat of that morning's kitchen criticism. "Mark, I told you yesterday that your neck was filthy, and you still haven't washed it!" Why hadn't I told him how much I liked his new shirt?

"Robert," that voice of mine persisted in my ears, "if you had come home at a decent hour last night, you could have got up this morning in time to pack your own lunch." I had forgotten about the party invitation Bob had turned down last week in order to visit his grandparents. And the breakfast in bed he had prepared when I had a sore throat.

"Whose turn was it to take out the garbage? . . . Who left the lights on in the basement?" Clearly, I had not hugged my children that day. And I wasn't really certain about the day before, either.

Feeling more like a monster than a mother, I decided to find out how other parents would respond to the question that had shaken me. So, at our next parents' group meeting at the school, I printed DID YOU HUG YOUR CHILD TODAY? in huge, capital letters on a blackboard that was in plain view, and waited for the reaction. Nearly everybody "changed lanes," pretending not to see the question.

Finally, prodded by the few parents who dared to face themselves, we spent the next two hours being scrupulously—and sometimes painfully—honest. Almost all of us admitted that we had not hugged our children that day; in fact, many of us came to see that hugging was not our general style. We were quick to criticize our children, but slow to compliment them. We often admired them, but seldom expressed our admiration. Bit by bit, we uncovered three reasons why our behavior as mothers and fathers failed to demonstrate the real feeling we have for our children:

1. A surprising number of us don't know how to hug. Some still think that a hug is simply an embrace. Not so! I came to realize that I hug Bob when I prepare broccoli with the lemon sauce that he loves. And Mark gets hugged every time his father saves the sports section of the paper when our young mountain climber is away camping. We concluded that a tone of voice can be a hug. So can a smile, a wink, a squeeze of the hand, a rumpling of hair, a whispered "good luck," an arm across the shoulder, a note on the pillow.

2. We may be afraid to hug. Some parents, especially fathers, seem embarrassed by any show of emotion. Even more, however, they are afraid of "spoiling" their children with praise. Parents often worry about children developing an inflated opinion of themselves, but I have yet to talk with a psychiatrist, psychologist or social worker who doesn't say that a deflated opinion, a weak ego, is the prevalent problem.

3. We don't always see any "huggable" qualities. We have no problem hugging our soft, cuddly babies, of course, but babies don't transer grime from their hands to a towel and call it washing. Or embarrass their parents in front of company. Or tie up the phone all night. Unmade beds, laundry-strewn floors, and deafening rock music are

seldom huggable. Small wonder, then, that we parents sometimes become so irate that we can't see the goodness for the "badness."

Fortunately, there are ways to train our eyes so that we behold our children with appreciation and can hug them. One comes from Professor Marie Hughes, recently retired from the University of New Mexico, who over the years encouraged teachers to send a note home every week praising something each child had done. Sometimes the praise came easily: "Tony finished his sixth book this month; we are all proud of him!" Or, perhaps, "Maria was elected class president on Monday; she is a fine leader!"

But the child who is hardest to hug usually needs the hugging most. Since Professor Hughes wanted every child to be appreciated every week, the teachers she was supervising sometimes had to dig deep to find a legitimate compliment. In the digging, however, they found qualities they might otherwise have overlooked. "Carlos is still having his troubles with reading, but he never lets failure discourage him. I admire his spirit!" Or, "We had a substitute teacher the first part of the week and Lola was very helpful to her. She deserves extra thanks for her kindness."

Adapting the Hughes approach provides a way for parents to give a daily—not just a weekly—hug. To be sure, it may be hard to find anything to compliment, but we can if we dig deeper.

There is a second technique for hugging children: Be as courteous with your children as you are with adults. Does that sound elementary? It isn't. Few of us would talk to our friends without observing the amenities that we routinely deny our children. "Stand up straight." No tact. "Have you taken a good look at how that sweater looks on you? It's two sizes too tight." No sensitivity, either.

My third technique for squeezing out a hug occurred to me when I was at my wit's end with Bob. After telling a good friend that my son had become "thoroughly inconsiderate, disagreeable and disorganized," I paused for breath. Before I could continue my litany, she said, "But Bob is such a generous boy, and he's completely undemanding. I wish my Nancy could be more like him, instead of always asking for a new 'something'."

"Don't be too hard on Nan," I urged. "I've never heard that child say an unkind word about anyone. She's pure honey." Suddenly, I realized: The way to admire your own children is to imagine they are someone else's for the moment. This fresh perspective is likely to produce something huggable every time!

A parent who has lost a child acquires a permanent change in perspective—a viewpoint that offers a lasting message for every mother and father. "Today, when I see parents impatient or tired or bored with their children, I wish I could say to them, 'But they are alive, think of the wonder of that!' " A mother named Frances Gunther wrote those words. Her son, John Gunther, Jr., had died of brain cancer when he was only seventeen. "Never," she declared, "have I felt the wonder and beauty and joy of life so keenly as now in my grief that Johnny is not here to enjoy them."

In her epilogue to *Death Be Not Proud,* the book by John Gunther about their son's fifteen-month fight to live, this mother implores those who still have sons and daughters to "embrace them with a little added rapture and a keener awareness of joy."

I intend to commit her words to heart. Any parent who does will never have to change lanes again when confronted with the question: "DID YOU HUG YOUR CHILD TODAY?"

CIPHER IN THE SNOW
By Jean Mizer Todhunter

It started with tragedy on a biting cold February morning. I was driving behind the Milford Corners bus as I did most snowy mornings on my way to school. It veered and stopped short at the hotel, which it had no business doing, and I was annoyed as I had to come to an unexpected stop. A boy lurched out of the bus, reeled, stumbled, and collapsed on the snowbank at the curb. The bus driver and I reached him at the same moment. His thin, sallow face was white even against the snow.

"He's dead," the driver whispered.

It didn't register for a minute. I glanced quickly at the scared young faces staring down at us from the school bus. "A doctor! Quick! I'll phone from the hotel . . ."

"No use, I tell you he's dead." The driver looked down at the boy's still form. "He never even said he felt bad," he muttered, "just tapped me on the shoulder and said, real quiet, 'I'm sorry, I have to get off at the hotel.' That's all. Polite and apologizing like."

The school, the giggling, shuffling morning noise quieted as the news went down the halls. I passed a huddle of girls. "Who was it? Who dropped dead on the way to school?" I heard one of them half whisper, "Don't know his name; some kid from Milford Corners," was the reply.

It was like that in the faculty room and the principal's office. "I'd appreciate your going out to tell the parents," the principal told me. "They haven't a phone, and anyway, somebody from school should go there in person. I'll cover your classes."

"Why me?" I asked. "Wouldn't it be better if you did it?"

"I didn't know the boy," the principal admitted levelly. "And in last year's sophomore personalities column I noted that you were listed as his favorite teacher."

I drove through the snow and cold down the bad canyon road to the Evans place and thought about the boy, Cliff Evans. His favorite teacher! Why, he hasn't spoken two words to me in two years! I could see him in my mind's eye all right, sitting back there in the last seat in my afternoon literature class. He came in the room by himself and left by himself. "Cliff Evans," I muttered to myself, "a boy who never talked." I thought a minute. "A boy who never smiled. I never saw him smile once."

The big ranch kitchen was clean and warm. I blurted out my news somehow. Mrs. Evans reached blindly toward a chair. "He never said anything about bein' ailing."

His stepfather snorted. "He ain't said nothin' about anything since I moved in here."

Mrs. Evans got up, pushed a pan to the back of the stove, and began to untie her apron. "Now hold on," her husband snapped. "I got to have breakfast before I go to town. Nothin' we can do now anyway. If Cliff hadn't been so dumb, he'd have told us he didn't feel good."

After school I sat in the office and stared bleakly at the records spread out before me. I was to close the boy's file and write his obituary for the school paper. The almost bare sheets mocked the effort. "Cliff Evans, white, never legally adopted by stepfather, five half-brothers and sisters." These meager strands of information and the list of D grades were about all the records had to offer.

Cliff Evans had silently come in the school door in the morning and gone out the school door in the evenings, and that was all. He had never belonged to a club. He had never played on a team. He had never held an office. As far as I could tell, he had never done one happy, noisy kid thing. He had never been anybody at all.

How do you go about making a boy into a zero? The grade school records showed me much of the answer. The first and second grade teachers' annotations read "sweet, shy child"; "timid but eager." Then the third grade note had opened the attack. Some teacher had written in a good, firm hand, "Cliff won't talk.

Uncooperative. Slow learner." The other academic sheep had followed with "dull"; "slow-witted"; "low IQ." They became correct. The boy's IQ score in the ninth grade was listed at 83.

But his IQ in the third grade had been 106. The score didn't go under 100 until the seventh grade. Even timid, sweet children have resilience. It takes time to break them.

I stomped to the typewriter and wrote a savage report pointing out what education had done to Cliff Evans. I slapped a copy on the principal's desk and another in the sad, dog-eared file; slammed the file; and crashed the office door shut as I left for home. But I didn't feel much better. A little boy kept walking after me, a boy with a peaked face, a skinny body in faded jeans, and big eyes that had searched for a long time and then had become veiled.

I could guess how many times he'd been chosen last to be on a team, how many whispered child conversations had excluded him. I could see the faces and hear the voices that said over and over, "You're dumb. You're dumb. You're just a nothing, Cliff Evans."

A child is a believing creature. Cliff undoubtedly believed them. Suddenly it seemed clear to me. When finally there was nothing left at all for Cliff Evans, he collapsed on a snowbank and went away. The doctor might list "heart failure" as the cause of death, but that wouldn't change my mind.

We couldn't find 10 students in the school who had known Cliff well enough to attend the funeral as his friends. So the student body officers and a committee from the junior class went as a group to the church, looking politely sad. I attended the service with them and sat through it with a lump of cold lead in my chest and a big resolve growing in me.

I've never forgotten Cliff Evans or that resolve. He has been my challenge year after year, class after class. Each September, I look up and down the rows carefully at the unfamiliar faces. I look for veiled eyes or bodies slouched into a seat in an alien world. "Look, kids," I say silently, "I may not do anything else for you this year, but not one of you is going out of here a nobody. I'll work or fight to the bitter end doing battle with society and the school board, but I won't have one of you leaving here thinking yourself into a zero."

Most of the time—not always, but most of the time—I've succeeded.*

This story is also available on 16mm and video.** It is excellent to use for staff development with teachers and for parent meetings. I also use it with students after I have established a good rapport with them, and they have some background in self-esteem work. I use it in conjunction with the I.A.L.A.C. story. Some of the questions I use in a follow-up discussion are:

- What were some of the contributing factors to Cliff's death?
- What could the family, school, and community have done to help Cliff?
- How can we help the Cliffs we meet?

- How can we help a child express his inner conflicts?
- What are some specific strategies we can use to help a child improve his self-concept?
- Most children don't die when they are confronted with the kind of life Cliff led. What happens to them?

Another film I use to reinforce the importance of self-esteem is entitled *Johnny Lingo*. This comes from the story "Johnny Lingo and the Eight-Cow Wife," by Patricia McGerr. The story appeared in *Woman's Day* magazine, November 1965, and is also available in 16mm and video from Britannica Educational Corporation. Just as Cliff's self-esteem was destroyed, a young girl who lives on an island in the South Pacific is told by her father and then the whole village that she is nothing. And that is exactly how she acts. Then Johnny Lingo comes to bargain for a wife and chooses her. He pays eight cows for her—more than anyone has ever paid for a wife on the island. At the end of the movie there is an amazing transformation in her appearance and behavior. The trader asks Johnny what happened. Johnny tells him that in her father's hut the young girl was nothing, but that he had loved her since they were children and she was always beautiful to him. In paying eight cows for her he showed her and the village that she had worth. Johnny says that the most important thing

---

* "Cipher in the Snow," by Jean Mizer Todhunter, appeared in *Today's Education* (N.E.A. Journal), September-October 1975. Mrs. Todhunter, an education writer, former teacher, and guidance counselor, won first prize in the first Teachers' Writing Competition with this true story. Originally published in 1964. Used by permission.
** Britannica Educational Corporation, 425 North Michigan Avenue, Chicago, Illinois 60611.

is how a woman feels about herself. (This is a powerful movie to show what can happen to a person who is constantly put down, and just as powerful in showing that self-esteem can be changed if only one person cares enough to make a difference in that person's life.)

An activity to follow the I.A.L.A.C. story would be the *Vulture Story,* by Dr. Sidney Simon. This activity deals with putting yourself down—how you do it and ways to correct it. *Negative Criticism,* by Dr. Simon, will give additional information to help you in carrying out these activities with your students.*

EYE CAN/I CAN
by Cherie Steuber

Building self-esteem by emphasizing and acknowledging a pupil's strengths and newly acquired skills.

Failure is a destructive spiral for all of us. For students at any age it can cause patterns and assumptions about one's inadequacies that may remain for a lifetime.

As teachers, we too often hear those two self-defeating words from our students "I can't." Breaking that

destructive cycle of those words may be possible through many methods, usually a combination of several.

Eye Can/I Can could be used as an addition to daily or weekly self-esteem building activities in the classroom or it can be used as a unit-type activity during the year. It is adaptable to a variety of classroom settings.

The core of this activity consists of the cans themselves. Use any type and size of can without sharp edges. Wrap each with a well-fitting piece of blank paper. Have each student decorate his/hers with large, colorful eyes. (His/her name printed in the back on the bottom might be a good idea.) Each can should then be placed in an area of easy access and workability within the room, whether this be on the students' desk or on a shelf, table, or ledge somewhere.

Introduction of the activity could be made in a variety of ways:
● Make the cans first, then describe the activity.
● Have a group discussion appropriate to the age level of the students about the things one can do, how we let ourselves think too much of the can'ts and, most of all, ways to change this.
● Have each pupil make a list of all the things they CAN do.
● Present the "Success . . ." poster to open discussion.

The class can then decide together (if not too young) some guidelines they will follow in using the cans, such as: who contributes "I can" notes; when the notes can be written and placed in the cans;

---

* All three of these books are available from Values Associates, 45 Old Mountain Road, Hadley, Massachusetts 01035. Permission was granted by Dr. Simon to use the adaptation of the I.A.L.A.C. story.

when the notes can be read, etc.

Two posters can be used along with this activity:

"Success comes in cans, not in cannots"
"They can who think they can"*

Adaptations, additions, and variations to this activity are encouraged.

For primary classrooms, the teacher may want to make a bulletin board using some key phrases on sentence strips. When a child has learned something new or achieved a goal, the teacher may just have him/her copy the phrase for more reinforcement.

Example:
I Can . . .

● Read words
● Read a book
● Count to 50
● Stand quietly in line
● Have good table manners
● Finish my work
● Be neat
● Play well with friends**

POOR WORM
by Ellen Campbell

Worm: It is a beautiful day. I feel great! I could climb the tallest tree.
Bug: Hey, worm. How do you expect to do your part for the balance of ecology if you won't do your share?

The IDEAL worm eats an average of one leaf a day . . . a BIG leaf. You are insignificant, but you'll never get your tiny job done if you don't hurry, HURRY, HURRY!
I always thought worms were all alike . . . lazy. Worms aren't too smart anyway. They'd forget where they were if their antennae weren't firmly attached.
Worm: But . . .
Bug: What's the matter, worm? Smile. And while I'm on the subject, worm, you don't look too great. You should take care of yourself. You can't put in a full day unless you take care of yourself. Worms sure have lousy dispositions.
Worm: But . . . But . . .
Bug: But . . . But . . . I didn't know worms stuttered!
Worm: Forget it. I don't feel so good. I'll curl up and go to sleep.
Bug: Didn't I tell you worms were lazy? You'll never get anywhere in the world or to worm heaven with that attitude.
Worm: (He slowly sinks before their eyes until finally he lies on the floor looking dejected and "squashed.")
Bug: Worms just don't listen. That worm is a loser. I tell him what is good for him and look at the thanks I get!

Pausing at the end of the dialogue for dramatic effect, the worm pops up and asks the children what changed him from such a happy worm to one who could hardly talk and barely muster the enthusiasm to lie on the floor. Usually the children are very critical of the bug and

* These may be ordered from Argus Communications, 7440 Natchez Avenue, Niles, Illinois 60648.
** Used by permission of Cherie Steuber.

insist that he allow the worm to talk more. At that time the teacher states simply that many people feel like the poor worm when faced with a domineering bug who ridicules what they think. Worms are then passed out to each child. Surprisingly the worms are received with compassion and tenderly cared for by most of the children. Whenever we need to mention another's feelings later, a mention of the worm is a speedy reminder of exactly what we mean.

To make the worms: Crochet a chain about 12 inches long from yarn. Double crochet in the first eight inches of the chain so that the crochet twists. Add eyes.*

I come in contact with many teachers as I teach university classes, seminars, workshops, and inservices. The talent I see exhibited by teachers never ceases to amaze me. I also see how loving and caring most teachers are, and know of many wonderful things going on in their classes. Mrs. Joyce Mims is such a teacher; I had the privilege of meeting her one summer when she took a reading class I taught. When she told me about her Teddy Bear Circle, I asked if she would like to share it with other teachers through my book. She very graciously consented and here is her activity.

THE TEDDY BEAR CIRCLE
By Joyce Summerrill Mims

The Teddy Bear Circle evolved from a need in my immediate family, which consists of three assertive, strong-minded people: myself, my husband, and my daughter. During family conferences called to discuss a problem, I noticed that at different times, one person would overpower the others and all feelings and thoughts would not surface from the others. Usually the slighted person would be our child, and mother and daddy would dominate and "solve" the problem, unaware of the lack of opportunity for input from the child. A new ground rule was introduced to the family conference, held at the dining room table, that whoever had the salt shaker was the only one who could speak. The person who called the conference would get the salt shaker first and talk as long as they wanted to and then pass it to the left. It was amazing how much more intelligent our solutions were and how much more understanding of one another's feelings and ideas we became. As a result of each person having the time and opportunity to be heard and not interrupted,

* Ellen Campbell, Decision-Making Skills Newsletter, Junior League of Phoenix, Inc. January 1978. Used with permission.

the frustrations melted away and a new family tradition emerged. We now end the family conference with a three-way hug.

This conference process naturally evolved to my classroom family. Any child with overwhelming problems can call for the Teddy Bear Circle. In the classroom the use of a teddy bear instead of a salt shaker was a serendipitous choice, but I must admit I feel now it was a guided choice as I watch each child lovingly caress and feel comfort with this object when it is time for their very own moment of truth.

The whole class sits in a circle. On a nice day the circle is outside in the grass under a tree. I speak only twice, once at the beginning and again at the end. I usually open by saying, "Tell us about your problem and how does it make you feel?" I hand the teddy bear to the child with the concern. When the first child has completely finished, the teddy bear is passed to the left. Each person, when receiving the teddy bear, may speak to the first person's problem or choose not to speak at all. The teddy bear continues around the circle until it reaches the first child again. I then ask, "How do you feel now?" Usually the child has been enriched from the caring and the solutions his classmates have presented. Rarely does the teddy bear make a second round for the same person's problem.

With this process each child has the opportunity to express his feelings, thoughts, and ideas while listening to the concerns and options offered by others. The important ingredient to the circle is the UNINTERRUPTED time each individual has while he possesses the teddy bear.

I have found that the Teddy Bear Circle promotes caring, kindness, openness, and social thinking skills, and, during the process, every participant gains a sense of worth and security.

As in our family conference we do not end the classroom Teddy Bear Circle with a thirty-way hug—but it might not be a bad idea.*

THE READING CONTRACT

When I left my fourth-graders and became a reading specialist with sixth-, seventh-, and eighth-graders, I was shocked at their lethargic, apathetic attitude toward reading. I would prepare lessons for them, and they would not even look at their reading material. Then I realized I had students not so much with reading problems but with self-concept problems. They did not believe that they could read! Dr. William Glasser in *Control Theory in the Classroom* writes of children coming to school with "pictures" in their heads that they are learners. He says that when these pictures are erased, it is very difficult to replace them. Dr. George Spache in *Reading for the Disadvantaged* cites research that there is a higher correlation between reading and self-concept than between reading and intelligence. I can vouch for that with my students. They were bright young people, but the lights had gone out on reading. My job was to get those lights

---

* Joyce Summerrill Mims, second-grade teacher, Curiel School, Eloy, Arizona.

back on. I incorporated lessons on self-esteem into my reading program. I used books and activities. Two of the books I used were *See You at the Top,* by Zig Ziglar, and *Go for It!* by Judy Zerafa. I employed a variety of materials and techniques in teaching reading. I continued to study the students. Then I realized they did not know where they stood in their learning process. They had not seen reading scores. They just knew they were in the "dumb" class for poor readers. I decided to share these scores with them and do some goal setting with them. Here is my plan, complete with contract.

How to Use the Goal Sheet

1. Put students' reading test scores from previous spring on sheet.
2. Give a goal sheet to each student face down. Tell them this information is private. It is their choice whether or not they want to share their scores with others. I've found that many students are seeing test scores for the first time. It seems significant to them that if they are going to be interested in doing well on tests, they need to be given this information.
3. Explain what the scores mean. Take time to explain that this is only one test score and is not indicative of their total reading picture. Explain that it is important for them to do their very best on each test, in other words, to put testing in its proper perspective.
4. Help students make realistic goals of what they would like to score on the next reading test. Record it on the goal sheet.

5. To be impartial, the teacher might predict two years' growth for each student.
6. During the school year, use a reading test that is not sacred to the testing program of your school district so the students can see their scores improve. I utilized only the reading-comprehension part of the test I used. This experience also helps students overcome their fear of testing.
7. After the teacher scores the reading test, let each student put his or her own score on the goal sheet. Students can compare the most recent score with past scores and see the progress they are making. This involves them in the testing aspect in a meaningful way.
8. In the spring, after the district test has been taken and scored, let them record their scores on their goal sheets.

How to Use the Contract

When I show the students the goal sheet the first time, I give each of them a contract, going over the three roles outlined in the contract. I have already signed it. I have them sign the contract. At the first grading period I make contact with as many parents as possible. Then I follow through with telephone calls and home visits. I found that many parents were looking at a test score on their child for the first time. They were interested in what the score represented. This is an opportunity to enlist parents' help in working with their children to improve reading skills, i.e., homework, visits to library, attitude toward school and reading. The whole purpose of the goal sheet and contract is to involve the student and the parent in the learning process.

Paid for from:
AOD Program Funds
Eau Claire Area School District
500 Main Street
Eau Claire, WI 54701

GETTING IT TOGETHER
Reading Contract

The TEACHER will:
1. Give individualized and small-group instruction, using materials at a level suited for student to master reading skills needed.
2. Provide practice in many reading materials to reinforce reading skills being taught.
3. Help student to experience success in reading according to his/her ability.
4. Provide assignments in reading for student to practice skills in reading during times other than just the reading period in the classroom.
5. Correct and grade assignments promptly.
6. Make student aware of his/her progress.
7. Re-evaluate student's progress regularly and readjust program as needed.
8. Communicate with parent when necessary and be available to parents.

The STUDENT will:
1. Exhibit an eagerness and willingness to learn to read.
2. Be respectful and attentive during teacher instruction time.
3. Work independently to complete an assignment given in class.
4. Accept responsibility for his/her own learning.
5. Be present each day unless ill.
6. Come to school rested and with an attitude of doing his/her best.
7. Be willing to do reading assignments at home.

The PARENT will:
1. Send the student to school with respect and desire for education.
2. Stress with student the importance of learning to read.
3. Cooperate with teacher to uphold standards of behavior conducive to a good learning atmosphere.
4. Have time set aside at home in the evenings for student to read, do homework, and read to younger children to teach them listening habits.
5. Cut down on amount of time television is watched in evening. Plan certain times for viewing and then turn off television.
6. See that student gets enough rest so he/she will be alert at school each day.
7. Communicate with school when there is a problem, so ALL can work together for progress of student.
8. Attend parent-teacher conferences and know what student is accomplishing in reading.
9. Provide books, magazines, newspapers, trips to library, and time to discuss these ideas from reading with the family.

Current Reading Status_____ Anticipated Year-end Reading Status_____
(Place reading score here.)

Student   Parent   Teacher

_____   _____   _____

SETTING READING GOALS FOR MYSELF

Reading Score Fall 19__	Teacher's Prediction	Other Testing	Student's Prediction Spring 19__	Reading Score
				8.8
				7.8
				6.8
				5.8
				4.8

On the day I presented this lesson on goal setting to my students, I took all the time needed to explain the testing, their test scores, and what was needed to improve their test scores, and, much more important, to improve their reading ability. I closed the lesson with a very special film, *Crossbar,* from Learning Corporation (see film section of book). I could have used other films like *The Emmett Smith Story* and *John Baker's Last Race* from Britannica (see film section of book). I wanted my students to see real people with real obstacles setting goals and achieving them. Later I would show them *A Desk for Billie* from N.E.A. (see film section of book). This is a true story about a young migrant girl who wanted to go to school and learn to read more than anything in the world. Her story is highly motivational for students.

Some of the stories that ensued provided an interesting aftermath of this lesson. Some students asked if they could re-take a test. "I didn't really try before; I just put down any answer." I had to reply that they could not take that test again, but that another would be given soon. After the first test following the goal-setting class, some of the students stayed behind to wait while I graded their tests on the computer. Their chins nearly rested on the top of my head as I graded and they watched the computer screen—then let out a whoop when they saw their scores come up. They had become involved in their own learning!

In case you think I am the Warm Fuzzy Lady totally immersed in affective education to the exclusion of a strong academic program—I have misled you. Students who do not have the cognitive skills they need to succeed in life are not going to feel good about themselves. They need to be held to high standards of excellence in academics. And we as teachers need to be prepared to teach to excellence. We need to provide for individual differences, and see that every student has a chance to succeed. This is why I share with you one of my techniques for teaching reading.

Ah Ha! Principle

For many years I watched my fourth-grade students struggle with the concepts of multiplication and long division. To some they came easily, while others viewed them with a heavy heart. Believing in a humane environment for my students and wanting all of them to experience success, I started using the Ah ha! principle.

I knew that all students had their own timing for learning. I talked to them about this timing. I asked if they had all learned to walk at the same time. Laughing, they would say, "Oh, no!" I asked if they had gotten a report card in their home stating that they failed walking if they had not learned to walk at a certain time. They found this analogy very funny. I used another example of learning to talk. After the point was made, I asked them about learning to read and doing math. Does it make sense that all of us are going to learn these things at the same time? The lights went on all over the room. They got it!

I taught the students to appreciate and have tolerance for their own timing. I called it the Ah ha! principle.

I told them, "When you get it (whatever concept is being taught), you say 'Ah ha!' and we will stop to celebrate your Ah ha! time. Each of you will have a different Ah Ha! time, and that is right and normal."

For a student who seemed discouraged, I would hug him and say, "It's not your Ah ha! time, but it will come, and I will help you. There is nothing wrong with you. Your Ah ha! time will come in its own good time."

As I discussed this principle with my students, they seemed relieved. We got on with learning in a more relaxed atmosphere. I hope I taught them an awareness and appreciation for their differences. I hope out there in life, they are still celebrating their uniqueness.

There Are Always Choices

The teenage suicide rate is very high in this country. One of the reasons people choose to commit suicide is that they feel they have no other options. They feel that they are at the end of their rope. Many of our students feel helpless, hopeless, and powerless. Following is an activity I learned somewhere along the way and adapted for an activity with junior high students. Using reading material and other activities to explore the concept that there are always choices, I use it as a culminating activity.

I tell the students to write down a problem or a challenge they have at that particular moment. Then I have them brainstorm as many options as they can and write them underneath the problem. I model one at the board, and we work through it as a group before they do this as an individual activity. I usually choose a frivolous topic like "I do not want to wash my clothes." Then we explore all of our options, i.e., wear dirty clothes, buy new ones, etc. We usually come up with six to eight ideas. Then we look at these options and discuss their feasibility. If we rule out all of the options and finally wash our clothes, we can see that it was a choice. We did have options.

I then give the students a chance to work through some of their own problems with this plan. I walk around the class while they are doing this and let them share with me if they so desire. Later I talk to them about taking this technique into the real world when things get rough, and using it to explore their options. I remind them that things always change. There is always another day and another opportunity. I talk to them about having more than one plan. If you have only Plan A and things fall through, you feel stuck. You have to be flexible and go to Plan B, and maybe to Plan C. I like to feel that these little lessons help them see that they have more control in their lives than they may have realized.

Journal Writing

Journal writing is an important component of the interest center on self-esteem. According to the grade level, appropriate writing materials were selected, i.e., journal notebooks, a sheet of construction paper folded over and sheets of paper tucked inside and secured with a paper clip, etc. Then some guidelines were established with the students. They could write about anything. I did not correct them for grammar or spelling. (However, in responding to the journals, I modeled correct spelling, grammar, etc. Several years later one student told me that this had been very helpful to her in learning to spell.) They could share their journals with me or not share, as they chose. I would respond to their journal writing if they so wished. We would have a certain time to write in class, and I would collect the journals of those who wanted me to answer them. We talked about privacy. No one would read their journal unless they decided to share their work. If they wanted to talk to me about something they did not wish to write in their journal, I would be available for a conference.

Some students had a hard time getting started. For those students I provided a list of possible journal topics. This list would include some sentence stems like this:

> Today I feel happy about . . .
> When I was little, I . . .
> I wish I could learn to . . .
> Television is . . .
> I am proudest of . . .
> Friends are . . .
> When I feel afraid, I . . .
> Music is . . .

I read of a state that gave seniors a writing test to determine their proficiency in language skills, i.e., writing, grammar, etc. When the tests were graded they were amazed at what the students wrote. They wrote of problems with drugs, thoughts of suicide, and other problems that teenagers have today. Psychologists were brought in to examine these writings and to see what they could make of them. I thought it so sad that students had to use a writing test to express their thoughts and feelings. Students have a lot inside of them. Journal writing is a way for them to get these feelings out and perhaps deal with them.

Some students will go on from this journal-writing experience in school to keeping a journal for life. One of my students who has continued this practice into her college years told me that her journal writing starts, "Dear Mrs. Hartline." Of course, I haven't kept a journal with her since junior high, but she says she still enjoys writing to me.

I-Messages

This is a good technique for teachers to teach students. It will help in creating a safe, happy environment in the classroom. I-messages are self-expressions that enable you and the students to express feelings and deal with inappropriate behavior without putting judgments on others. The opposite of an I-message is a you-message. You-messages are always put-downs. I-messages are never put downs. Here is an example:

You-message:
 "You jerk, you spilled pop on my new dress!"
I-message:
 "Julie, I don't like it when you spill pop on me. Would you please try to be more careful?"

The term I-messages was developed by Thomas Gordon. I want to refer you to his book, *T.E.T., Teacher Effectiveness Training*, for a comprehensive understanding of this technique. Then I would refer you to *S.T.E.T. (Systematic Training for Effective Teaching) Teacher's Handbook,* pp. 95-105, for a good plan for teaching this in a classroom.* *S.T.E.T.* also contains many strategies and activities for creating a humane environment in the classroom.

The last two pages of this section, "My Thoughts to You" and "I Love You Because" can be used to go inside greeting cards students make for their parents and others.

* This book is available through American Guidance Service, Publishers' Building, P. O. Box 99, Circle Pines, MN 55014-1796.

MYSELF

I have to live with myself, and so
I want to be fit for myself to know.
I want to be able, as days go by,
Always to look myself straight in the eye.
I don't want to stand, with the setting sun,
And hate myself for the things that I've done.
I want to go out with my head erect,
I want to deserve all men's respect.
For here in the struggle for fame and self
I want to be able to like myself.
I don't want to look at myself and know
I'm bluster, a bluff, and empty show.
I can never hide myself from me;
I see what others may never see.
I know what others may never know,
I never can fool myself, and so,
Whatever happens, I want to be
Self-respecting and conscience-free.

—Author unknown

My Thoughts To You

To:_____

I love you because:_____
_____
_____

I like you because:_____
_____
_____

I admire you because:_____
_____
_____

I respect you because:_____
_____
_____

Remember when:_____
_____
_____

From: _____

I LOVE you because

11
RESOURCES

A & M Records, Inc.
P. O. Box 118
Hollywood, California 90028

   Title: "Free to Be a Family" (20 songs & stories), Marlo Thomas & Friends

Abbey Press
St. Neinrad, Indiana 47577

This is a good source for motivational and inspirational posters.

Advocacy Press
P.O. Box 236
Santa Barbara, California 93102

   Titles: *Choices,* activity book, junior/senior high girls

         Challenges, activity book, junior/senior high boys

Affective Skill Development
P. O. Box 67001
Lincoln, Nebraska 68506
402-423-1623

Connie Dembrowsky has written and published two dynamic programs to develop self-esteem and internal motivation. They are not merely a collection of activities but task-analyzed, scoped, and sequenced curricula. Schools on four continents use these materials in a variety of courses: high-risk; substance abuse prevention; special education; gifted-talented; leadership training; and as a graduation requirement for all students. There are two levels available—one for middle schools/junior high, and one for high school. The middle school/junior high curriculum is not a prerequisite for the high school program.

Middle School/Junior High Level

Title: *Self-Esteem*

This highly structured course helps develop self-esteem through concrete activities. Ideally suited to younger adolescents, these 85 lessons help students build strong, realistic, positive self-images. Becoming increasingly more self-directed, they take greater responsibility for their actions and set goals for positive growth. Included is an optional eight-session Parent Program to provide parents with the skills to interact more effectively with their teenagers during those often trying adolescent years.

Curriculum Materials

1 Teacher's Manual . . . . .371 pages
1 Appendix . . . . .177 pages
1 Student Activity Book . . . . . . 246 pages
1 Parent Leader's Manual . . . . .150 pages
1 Parent Activity Book . . . . .79 pages

High School Level

Title: *Personal and Social Responsibility*

This experientially based, 82-lesson curriculum develops the students' sense of personal responsibility to be successful in their own lives while challenging them to exercise their social responsibility to others. Students deal successfully with "real world" choices as they learn specific steps to gain more influence and control over what happens to them in life. An optional ten-session Parent Program is included to help parents assist young adults in assuming self-responsibility.

Curriculum Materials

2-Volume Teacher's Manual . .539 pages
1 Student Activity Book . . . . . .400 pages
1 Parent Leader's Manual . . . . .144 pages
1 Parent Activity Book . . . . .65 pages
2 Color Video Tapes . . . . 25 min.

American Guidance Service
Publishers' Building
P. O. Box 99
Circle Pines, Minnesota 55014-1796

Titles: *Developing Understanding of Self and Others*

DUSO-1, Revised, gr. K-2

DUSO-2, Revised, gr. 3-4

Special Needs Books (set of 6), gr. K-4

Friendship/Peer Books (set of 6), gr. 1-4

S.T.E.T. (Systematic Training for Effective Teaching)

Teacher's Handbook and *Teacher's Resource Book* (2 books)
Excellent activities for classroom instruction.

Applied Skills Press
200 S. Bemiston, Suite 202
St. Louis, Missouri 63105

Title: *The Encyclopedia of Ice Breakers,* warm-up activities

Argus Communications
7440 Natchez Avenue
Niles, Illinois 60648

This is a good source for motivational and inspirational posters.

Arista Records, Inc.
Arista Building
6 W. 57th Street
New York, New York 10019

Titles: "The Greatest Love of All," George Benson

"That's What Friends Are For," Dionne Warwick

Celestial Arts
231 Adrian Road
Millbrae, California 94030

Title: I Am Me, poster by Virginia Satir

Center for Human Development
3702 Mt. Diablo Blvd.
Lafayette, California 94549

Title: *Tribes,* Jeanne Gibbs
Activities in affective education/cooperative learning.

Children's Press
5540 North Cumberland Avenue
Chicago, Illinois 60656

Titles: *Let's Talk About Series,* Joy Wilt Berry, gr. preschool–2

The Survival Series for Kids, Joy Wilt Berry, gr. 3+

Teach Me About Series, Joy Wilt Berry, gr. preschool–2

What Does It Mean? (12 books of feelings), gr. preschool–2

Understanding Myself Picture Books, gr. preschool–3

A New Values Series, gr. preschool–2

Columbia Records, C.B.S. Records, Inc.
51 W. 52nd Street
New York, New York 10019

Title: "When a Child Is Born," Johnny Mathis

Creative Educational Materials
P. O. Box 18344
West St. Paul, Minnesota 55118-0344

Titles: *Dealing with Feelings,* activity book, gr. 2–6

The Month-to-Month Me, activity book, gr. 4–6

I Am Special, activity book, gr. 1-4

Marvelous Me, activity book, gr. K–3

Feelings About Friends, activity book, gr. 3–6

Goal Getters, activity book, gr. 3–6

Good source for banners, awards, and T–shirts.

Creative Teacher Publications
P. O. Box 41
Williston Park, New York 11596

Titles: *My Family History* (English & Spanish), gr. 2–6

Happy to Be Me, activity cards, different levels, gr. K–7

Happy to Be Me (English & Spanish), award pads

T. S. Denison & Company, Inc.
9601 Newton Avenue South
Minneapolis, Minnesota. 55431

This is a good source for awards.

Difference Makers, Inc.
P. O. Box 2115
Delmar, California 92014-1415

Title: *Who I Am Makes a Difference*

Source for blue ribbon awards

Educational Activities, Inc.
Box 392
Freeport, New York 11520

Titles: *Working the Anger Out Without Hurting,* by Jack Hartmann

Won't You Be My Friend, by Patty Zeitlin and Marcia Berman

I'm a Very Special Person, by Del Baroni

These are records of self-esteem songs.

Educational Insights
19560 S. Rancho Way
Dominguez Hills, California 90220

Titles: *All About Me,* activity book, gr. 2–3

Me, Myself and I, activity book, gr. 2–3

Values, activity book, gr. 4+

Decision-Making, activity book, gr. 4+

Personal Skills, activity book, gr. 4+

Social Skills, activity book, gr. 4+

Educational and Training Services, Inc.
P. O. Box 1532
Santa Cruz, California 95061

Titles: *Building Self-Esteem,* curriculum guide K-8, Dr. Robert Reasoner

Self-Esteem, A Classroom Affair, vols. 1 & 2, Michele and Craig Borba, gr. K-6

Elektra/Asylum Records
962 No. La Cienega Blvd.
Los Angeles, California 90069

Titles: "Flowers Are Red," Harry Chapin Living Room Suite

"Cat's in the Cradle," anthology of Harry Chapin

Epic Records/ C.B.S., Inc.
1801 Century Park West
Los Angeles, California

    Title: "The Man in the Mirror," Michael Jackson

Good Apple, Inc.
Box 299
Carthage, Illinois 62321

    Titles: All About Me (poster), K-12, My Family History (poster), gr. 3-8,
               Friendship (poster), gr. 2-6, About Me, Myself & I, (poster), primary;
               About My Birthday (poster), gr. 2-6,

    Activity Books: *Caring, Feeling, Sharing, Belonging, Appreciating, Coping,*
                    Loving,Communicating, Choosing, Relating, Living, Cooperating,
                    gr. 2-8; *Writing About My Feelings,* gr. 1-8; *Let's Learn About*
                    Magnificient Me, gr. preschool–2; *Let's Learn About Getting Along*
                    with Others, preschool-2

    Note Pads: Warm Fuzzy, Happy Gram, etc.

Hallmark Cards, Inc.
Kansas City, Missouri 64141

    Title: To Kids with Love

        Self-esteem greeting cards.

Hayes School Publishing Company, Inc.
321 Pennwood Avenue
Wilkinsburg, Pennsylvania 15221

    This is a good source for awards, certificates, bookmarks.

Hugs Unlimited
P. O. Box 4041
Huntington Beach, California 92605

    This is a good source for bumper stickers, buttons, stationery pads, sweat shirts,
    T-shirts, aprons, totes, badges, warm fuzzies, and books.

Incentive Publications, Inc.
3835 Cleghorn Avenue, Dept. 989
Nashville, Tennessee 37215-2532

    Titles: *The Me I'm Learning to Be,* activity book, gr. 4-7

From A-Z with Me, activity book, gr. l-3,

I've Got Me and I'm Glad, activity book, gr. 4-7,

People Need Each Other, activity book, gr. 4-7

School spirit and self-esteem bulletin boards

Innerchoice Publishing
P. O. Box 2476
Spring Valley, California 92077

Title: *Just Say I Know How,* a curriculum guide for saying no to drugs through self-esteem lessons/activities, gr. 3-6

Insight Productions
1346 No. Columbia Avenue, Suite B
Glendale, California 91202

Title: "That Kid Can Fly," Michael Byers

This is a beautiful tape of self-esteem songs.

Institute of Living Skills
P. O. Box l46l
Fallbrook, California 92028

Titles: *Ready-Set-Grow Series, Teach-Me-About Program, The Survival Series for Kids Program, The You Can Program,* and more

This is the source for Joy Wilt and Marilyn Berry materials.

International Foundation
4325 Dick Pond Road , Hwy. 544
Myrtle Beach, South Carolina 29575

Titles: *Power of Positive Students,* Dr. William Mitchell

Learning to Positive, curriculum guide, grades K-4

Learning to Positive, curriculum guide, grades 5-8

Learning to Positive, curriculum guide, grades 9-12

Kid Love Unlimited
1825 Westcliff Drive, Ste. 126
Newport Beach, California 192660

Title: *Otto Series,* books for preschool, primary, teaching self-esteem.

Learning Works
P. O. Box 6187, Dept. LW
Santa Barbara, California 93111

Titles: *Dealing with Feelings,* activity sheets, gr. 2-6

Month-to-Month Me, activity sheets, gr. 4-6

I Am Special, activity sheets, gr. K-3

Goal Getters, activity sheets, gr. 3-6

Little, Brown and Company
34 Beacon Street
Boston, Massachusetts 02106

Title: *Great Thumbprint Drawing Book,* Ed Emberly

Live, Love, Laugh
P. O. Box 9432
San Diego, California 92109

Title: *More Teachable Moments,* curriculum guide for K-12

Mariposa Arts
P. O. Box 83695
Los Angeles, California 90083

Title: "Milk Shake Moustaches & Bubbly Bath," a cassette of self-esteem songs

Network Publications
1700 Mission Street, Suite 203
P. O. Box 1830
Santa Cruz, California 95061-1830

Title: *Family Life Education: Resources for the Elementary Classroom,* gr. 4-6

Nightingale-Conant
7300 North Lehigh Avenue
Chicago, Illinois 60648

Titles: "How to Build Your Child's Self-Esteem," Denis Waitley

"What do You Really Want for Your Children?" Dr. Wayne Dyer

"You're Nature's Greatest Miracle," Bob Moawad (ages 5-9)

"You've Got What It Takes," Bob Moawad (ages 10-13)

"Unlocking Your Potential," Bob Moawad (ages 14 & up)

"The Psychology of Self-Esteem," Dr. Nathaniel Branden

All of the above are audiocassettes. This company is a good source for tapes by Dr. Maxwell Maltz, Dr. Wayne Dyer, Zig Ziglar, Denis Waitley, Leo Buscaglia, Dr. Bernie Siegel, Dr. Gerald Jampolsky, Bob Moawad, Dr. Nathaniel Branden, Dr. Norman Vincent Peale, Dr. Robert Schuller, and others.

Palomares & Associates
P. O. Box 1517
Spring Valley, California 92077

Titles: *Magic Circle,* activity guides prechool–sixth grade

Innerchange, program for junior high/high school

Peter Pan Industries
88 St. Francis Street
Newark, New Jersey 07105

Title: "When You Dream a Dream," Bob Schneider
This is a cassette of self-esteem songs.

Positive Action
P. O. Box 2347
321 Eastland
Twin Falls, Idaho 83303-2347

Title: *Positive Action,* curriculum guides for grades 1-6

Positive Life Attitudes of America
13642 Omega at Alpha
Dallas, Texas 75234

Titles: *See You at the Top,* Zig Ziglar, junior high/high school

I Can Course, elementary–high school curriculum materials

Price/Stern/Sloan Publishers, Inc.
360 N. La Cienega Blvd.
Los Angeles, California 90048

Titles: *My Own Book, My Personal Book, My Private Book,* and others.

Write-It-Yourself Books, by Dina Anastasio

This company is also the source for Wee Sing, cassettes of songs for children.

Project Pride
2530 East Broadway, Suite D
Tucson, Arizona 85716

  Title: *Project Pride,* curriculum guide K-8

Quest International
537 Jones Road
P. O. Box 566
Granville, Ohio 43023-0566

  Titles: *Skills for Living,* high school curriculum

  Skills for Adolesence, junior high curriculum

  Skills for Growing, K–fifth grade curriculum

R. C. A.
1133 Avenue of the Americas
New York, New York 10036

  Titles: "The Point," Nilsson
  This is the story and music of a little boy who is different.

  "Wind Beneath My Wings," Roger Whittaker

Research Press
Box 3177 Dept. H
Champaign, Illinois 61821

  Titles: *Skillstreaming the Elementary School Child: A Guide for Teaching*

  Prosocial Skills, elementary, Drs. McGinnis, Goldstein, Sprafkin, Gershaw

  Skillstreaming the Adolescent: A Structured Learning Approach to Teaching

  Prosocial Skills, Junior/Senior High, Drs. McGinnis, Goldstein, Sprafkin, Gershaw

Self-Esteem Seminars
17156 Palisades Circle
Pacific Palisades, California 90272

  Titles: *Self-Esteem in the Classroom: A Curriculum Guide,* K–college, Jack Canfield
  There are other self-esteem materials, videos, tapes, and workshops available through this source.

Siccone Foundation
2254 Union Street #1
San Francisco, California 94123

Title: *Responsibility: The Most Basic R,* curriculum guide, gr. 4-12, Frank Siccone

Teaching Resources Corporation
100 Boylston Street
Boston, Massachusetts 02116

Title: *It's Me: Building Self-Concepts Through Art,* June H. Campbell

Teaching Stuff
P. O. Box 9366, Dept. K
Glendale, California 91206-0366

Title: *Happy Thinking,* activity card book, gr. K-6

The Ungame Company
1440 South State College Boulevard
Building 2-D
Anaheim, California 92806

Titles: The Ungame (ages 5 and up)

The Pocket Size Ungame (kids' version)

The Pocket Size Ungame (all-age version)

Social Security (ages 6 and up)

Roll-A-Roll (ages 8 and up)

Thinking Caps
P. O. Box 17714
Phoenix, Arizona 85011

Title: *Stories Told from Beyond the Double Rainbow,* Elaine Hardt
         Little stories that teach big lessons.

Trend Enterprises, Inc.
P. O. Box 64073
St. Paul, Minnesota 55164

Titles: *Exploring Our Emotions* (bulletin board)

Myself & Others (bulletin board)

I'm a Winner (bulletin board)

Banners and Awards

Values Associates
45 Old Mountain Road
Hadley, Massachusetts 01035

Titles: *I Am Lovable and Capable (I.A.L.A.C.)*

Vulture

Negative Criticism

Meeting Yourself Halfway

Values Clarification (handbook of activities for teachers)

Caring, Touching, Feeling

Getting Unstuck

The above books were written by Dr. Sidney Simon.

Whitenwife Publications
149 Magellan Street
Capitola, California 95010

Titles: *Songs of Self-Esteem,* songbook and cassette tape

Nourishing Self-Esteem (book for parents)

The Art of Nurturing (book for parents & teachers)

Willow Run Community Schools
2171 E. Michigan Avenue
Ypsilanti, Michigan 48197

Title: *C.A.S.T.L.E.* (Creating a Safe Teaching & Learning Environment)
Many activities to use, K-6.

B. L. Winch & Associates/Jalmar Press
45 Hitching Post Drive, Bldg. 25
Rolling Hills Estates, California 90274-4297

Titles: *Esteem Builders,* K-8, curriculum guide, Dr. Michele Borba

Project Self-Esteem, a parent involvement project for elementary age children, Sandy McDaniel/Peggy Bielen

T.A. for Tots, T.A. for Kids, T.A. for Teens

The Original Warm Fuzzy Tale, Claude Steiner

Songs of the Warm Fuzzy, All About Your Feelings, Communicating to Make Friends, gr. K-8, Dr. Lynn Fox

Social Acceptance: Key to Mainstreaming, gr. K–8, Dr. Lynn Fox

Unlocking Doors to Friendship, gr. 7–12, Dr. Lynn Fox

Value Tales, ages 3-12 (31 books and guide)

Wise Owl Publications
9910 South Main Street
Los Angeles, California 90028

Titles: *I Believe,* task cards, gr. 4-8

I Have Feelings! task cards, gr. 4-8

In Search of One's Self, task cards, gr. 4-8

Me! task cards, gr. 3-8

Word Resources
Educational Products Division
P. O. Box 2518
Waco, Texas 76702

Title: *Relationship Builders,* 156 activities and games for building relationships, two books, ages 4-8 and ages 8-12

Write 'Em Notes Publishing Company
Kennesaw, Georgia 30144

Title: Praise 'Em Notes (great motivational notes)

Zephyr Press
P.O. Box 13448
Tucson, Arizona 85732-3448

Titles: *Chrysalis,* Micki McKisson, gr. 4-12

How to Become an Expert, Gibbons and Keating, gr. 5-8

Joining Hands, Rahima Wade, gr. K-4

A Moving Experience, Teresa Benzwie, preschool-6

Zephyr Press is a source of a broad range of resources for creating a classroom centered around promoting self-esteem.

12
FILMS AND VIDEOS

Always use films for a specific purpose. Preview the film to be shown and make note of points to be drawn out with your students. Before presenting the film, create interest in it and point out things to observe. Watch the film with your students; this lets them know that you as the teacher value the lesson to be learned from it. ALWAYS have a follow-up discussion; elicit from the students what they learned from the film, how they felt about it, and how the lesson applies to their own lives.

Aims Instructional Media Services, Inc.
2820 W. 116 Pl., #203
Denver, Colorado 80234

Feeling Left Out. Divorce leaves many children with a temporary sense of isolation and depression. This film is designed to help children through this period of adjustment. (Grades 1-8)

Guidance—Does Color Really Make a Difference? Through the use of colored raincoats, hoods, and rain boots that represent different ethnic groups, children are seen walking home from school and playing in the rain. Their attitude and treatment of one another in different, yet parallel, social situations is portrayed. (Grades 1-5)

Guidance—Working with Others: Through the use of situation-type episodes, the students are asked to find answers to social situations pertaining to: Respect for race, the opposite sex, the handicapped, and allowing themselves to become involved in aiding others. (Grades 1-5)

I'm Somebody Special. Children learn they are already somebody worthwhile by being themselves. Indirect lessons on the worth and uniqueness of each person are revealed through the everyday lives of our children. (Grades 4-8)

Take a Look at Yourself. A fatherless youth expresses to his recreation director a hatred for policemen and authority. When his bicycle is stolen, he realizes police are valuable and important to people. When he discovers that the policeman who finds and returns his bicycle is his recreation director, he acquires a new sense of respect for law and order. (Grades 5-8)

There's Nobody Else Like You: Documents a class on a field trip to the zoo. During class discussion and during games at recess, viewers hear a zookeeper tell how he knows one animal from another, though they appear to be identical. Children discuss merits of difference and sameness. (Grades 1-6)

Ambrose Video Publishing, Inc.
381 Park Avenue South, Suite 1601
New York, New York 10016

The Bridge of Adam Rush. This story is set in the early 1800s. Adam moves from city life to his new stepfather's farm. Their shaky relationship is put to the test when they must build a bridge to remain solvent. (Elementary/Junior High)

Hewitt's Just Different. Willie is a preteen whose 16-year-old neighbor Hewitt is retarded. With his friend Hewitt's help, Willie makes the baseball team, and makes a choice between old friends and new ones. (Elementary/Junior High)

Home to Stay. This story is adapted from the novel *Grandpa and Frank* by Janet Majerus. While grandfather fights lapses into senility, his granddaughter fights her uncle's plan to place him in a nursing home. (Elementary/Junior High)

The Horrible Honchos. This story is based on the novel *Seventeenth Street Gang,* by Emily Neville, and deals with a new boy in the neighborhood harassed by a children's gang. Peer pressure leads to dangerous pranks. (Elementary/Junior High)

Me and Dad's New Wife. This story is based on the book *A Smart Kid Like You,* by Stella Pevsner. (Elementary/Junior High)

New York City Too Far from Tampa Blues. When his family moves from Tampa to Brooklyn, Tom forms a successful singing duo. As he begins to earn more and more money, his father, a proud man forced out on strike, becomes increasingly defensive. (Elementary/Junior High)

P. J. and the President's Son. One is the son of the president, one is a middle-class kid. In this updated version of *The Prince and the Pauper,* each learns about life in someone else's shoes, and appreciates his own lot more. (Elementary/Junior High)

You Don't Have to Die: Jason's Story. Jason Gaes, a cancer victim at age 6, was tired of books and programs about children who die of cancer. He wanted one about children who live. So at age 8, he wrote one himself. The real message is irrepressible hope. Most people are unaware of the dramatic improvement in chances for curing childhood cancer. It provides an excellent model for strength and family values. It can be used in schools to help kids verbalize their feelings and fears about illness. (Elementary/Junior High)

Barr Films
12801 Schabarum Avenue
P. O. Box 7878
Irwindale, California 91706-7878

Day in the Life of Bonnie Consolo. Bonnie Consolo was born without arms, yet leads a normal and productive life. Film follows her through a typical day as she cares for her home and family, and as she goes about her family routine, she shares with us her thoughts about life. (Grades 6-8)

Britannica Films & Video
425 North Michigan Avenue
Chicago, Illinois 60611

Cipher in the Snow. Story of a boy no one thought was important until his sudden death one snowy morning. Emphasizes concern for the needs of every child. (Grades 7-8) (Teachers, Parents)

Johnny Baker's Last Race. Story of a champion athlete with terminal cancer who was given only six months to live. His last race, the race for life, became his greatest— dedicating his life to the children he taught, making every child feel important, especially those who could never win. His example of selfless human devotion influenced hundreds of children. (Grades 6-8) (Teachers, Parents)

Johnny Lingo. A timeless Polynesian love story that shows how profoundly a person is affected by his feeling of self-worth and how others can influence these feelings. Filmed in a beautiful Hawaiian setting, it will never become dated by changing styles. Appropriate for all ages and wherever the building of self-worth is important. (Grades 4-8) (Teachers, Parents)

Nobody's Useless. With his knack for accomplishing seemingly impossible schemes and his tireless imagination, young Tom, self-proclaimed "great brain" and all-around bamboozler, helps a young boy whose leg is amputated realize that there are many ways people can use their natural talents and intelligence, and that the challenge of overcoming of a physical handicap can be met with humor and courage. (Grades 5-8)

Share It with Someone. Shows children how sharing can help develop and enrich relationships with other people. (Grades K-1)

The Emmett Smith Story. Story of a teacher and coach with a brain tumor who learns to walk again, and even run, against incredible odds. He inspires one of his students, who has been crushed in an automobile accident, to set goals for herself so that she will be able to walk again. (Grades 4-8)

This Is Me. Helps children understand and appreciate their capacities for self-expression. (Grades K-1)

Churchill Films
12210 Nebraska Avenue
Los Angeles, California 90025

Climb. The thoughts of two men transform a suspenseful rock-climbing film into a parable of living, of struggle, of independence and interdependence. (Grades 6-8)

I Am How I Feel. Raucous circus music and a young clown give lively pace to this film about feelings. Children express a variety of feelings: a skit pokes fun at one method of finding happiness; a section showing dogs and their feelings illustrates that different feelings are natural and desirable. Children talk about feeling frightened, angry, or lonely. (Grades K-6)

I Am How I Look. An exploration of how children view their physical self and how that relates to the whole self-image. A skit illustrates that not all people have the same ideas of how they should look, emphasizing the importance of differences for helping one develop a sense of self-identity and suggesting ways for liking oneself better. (Grades K-6)

I Am What I Know. A bumbling young professor introduces concept that an important part of what I am is what I know. A skit suggests a humorous way of knowing more: three children express unhappiness at things they don't know. Ways to feel better about one's attainments are illustrated. (Grades K-6)

I'm Feeling Alone. Begins with a song, "Everybody Has Feelings," and an animated sequence of children's faces. Illustrates situations in which children are lonely. Filmed experiences help children to talk about and understand their own feelings. (Grades K-4)

I'm Feeling Happy. Children in the film sing about and experience a number of things that cause people to feel happiness, like smelling and eating good things, a bubbly bath, waking up on a sunny morning, baking a cake, being helpful, and sharing a friendship. (Grades K-3)

I'm Feeling Sad. Begins with a song "Everybody Has Feelings," and an animated sequence of children's faces. Illustrates situations in which children are sad. (Grades K-4)

I'm Feeling Scared. What's there to be scared of? Children in this film illustrate their fears of worms and dogs, high diving boards, the principal's office, losing mother in the park, meeting new people, and dark alleyways. Some of the fears serve as protective warning and others are the child's own fears that are just as potent and need to be accepted and understood by others. (Grades K-3)

I'm Mad at Me. Film depicts children experiencing frustrating situations. The feeling evoked is one of being mad due to the frustrating events, where nobody outside the child is at fault. (Grades K-3)

The Giving Tree. Unselfishly, a tree offers itself to a boy for climbing, shade, and pleasure. As the boy grows, he wants different things from the tree. Life takes him away, but old age brings their relationship full circle. (Grades K-8)

The Hundred Penny Box. Story about Michael, his hundred-year-old great-great Aunt Dew, and his mother, and the "big ugly old box." The box holds a small sack with a hundred pennies, each a memory of a year of Aunt Dew's life. Michael liked to count the pennies and listen to the stories. His mother, burdened by the care of the failing old lady who disrupts the order of her house, wants to get rid of the box, but Michael is fiercely defiant. At story's end, Aunt Dew still has her box and memories. (Grades K-8)

To Try Again . . . and Succeed. The little eagle fears to fly but yearns to soar. With the help of one who cares, the eaglet tries and finally succeeds. Film illustrates the act of helping others in a format understandable to all ages. (Grades 5-8)

Coronet/MTI Film & Video
108 Wilmot Road
Deerfield, Illinois 60015

A Different Kind of Winning. Jody Flynn has recently moved to southern California from a small town in Ohio. Her father's company is sponsoring a skateboard contest and he insists that Jody enter. The competition is much tougher than in Ohio, and as Jody watches Sean Masters and Carmen Mendella, she is certain she doesn't stand a chance of winning. Mr. Flynn thinks differently. However, Jody teaches her father a different kind of lesson about winning. (Grades 4-8)

Angel and Big Joe. Angel, a fifteen-year-old migrant worker, has to make a difficult decision—whether or not to move and help his family in Arizona or stay in New Jersey and go into business with his newfound friend Joe, a telephone repairman. This is a beautiful story of friendship and loyalty to family, and is great for decision-making classes. (Grades 4-8)

Crossbar. Aaron Kornylo is determined to reach Olympic qualifications in the high jump despite having only one leg. Discouraged by his father, Aaron refuses to acknowledge his handicap. He jumps and clears the required height only to find the Olympic committee refusing his entry. Eventually he is allowed to compete, and as the competition narrows, he decides that winning isn't as important as "getting there." (Grades 4-8) (Teachers, Parents)

Every Day of Our Lives. Depicts the many ways people must have faith in each other in order to live in our society, whether we are mailing a letter or placing our lives in a surgeon's hands. (Grades 3-8)

Family of Strangers. Dominic Ginetti is a widowed father of two girls. Marie Mills is a divorced mother with one daughter. Their marriage brings the five individuals together as a family of strangers. Trouble begins at the beginning as the three girls are at one another during the wedding ceremony. But Dominic eases the tension through a gesture of love and the family of strangers take the first strides toward being a family of friends. (Grades 4-8)

Felipa: North of the Border. Felipa's family is Hispanic. Her story conveys a sense of the frustration felt by a person who does not understand the language of the place where she lives. As Felipa expresses it, "It's almost like being blind." (Grades 5-8)

Irene Moves In. Irene, a new girl in the neighborhood and school, has to gain acceptance. Prejudice and friendship are explored. Parents become involved in resolving the conflict. (Grades 3-8)

Little Brown Burro. A tale of a forlorn little donkey, belittled as useless, who comes to realize that by doing his best he can make his own special kind of contribution. His journey to self-confidence begins with his encounter with a desert rat named Omar, and they enter into a series of humorous and sometimes poignant adventures that illustrate the ingenuity of Omar and the vulnerability of the little donkey. (Grades K-8)

Miss Nelson Is Missing. Miss Nelson is an excellent teacher, but her class refuses to listen to her. One day she mysteriously fails to appear, and poisonous "Miss Swamp" takes over the class. The kids realize how much they like Miss Nelson and begin searching for her. Having taught her students a lesson, she (alias Miss Swamp) reappears as herself to a responsive class. (Grades K-5)

Morris, the Midget Moose. Scorned because his huge antlers crown a diminutive body, Morris is ridiculed during the annual challenge to the head moose. He meets Balsam, a moose with the opposite problem, and together the two learn to transform a weakness into an advantage. (Grades K-4)

The Pinballs. Three displaced children find themselves sharing the same foster home. They begin their relationship on angry terms, each disillusioned by past experiences. A pair of concerned foster parents provide an environment in which the three youngsters learn to care. (Grades 4-8)

Shopping Bag Lady. A study on values of compassion, tolerance, and empathy. The relationship between a young girl and an elderly woman derelict produces an awareness of what it's like to be old, to value people as individuals, and to not make snap judgments according to outward appearances. (Grades 4-8)

Snowbound. Two teenagers are snowbound—one the handsome football star and the other a girl who would be considered a wallflower. The story of their survival is a study of real strengths in human beings. (Grades 6-8)

Sunshine's on the Way. Bobba June Strang is a fifteen-year-old whose one ambition in life is to be a great jazz trombonist. Her mother doesn't quite understand her daughter. Bobba June helps the family by working part-time at the Sugar Hill Nursing Home, and she has successfully encouraged many of the patients to form a jazz band. One day, T. P. Jackson, a great jazz trombonist who happens to be Bobba June's idol, arrives at the home. He has had a stroke and is discouraged. Bobba June and the others at the home rally around him, and they all have a unique experience. (Grades 6-8) (Teachers, Parents)

That's My Name—Don't Wear It Out. In this contemporary story from Canada, a troublesome but sensitive adolescent befriends a deaf youngster. Both boys mature from this relationship. The older boy becomes less wary of involvement, and the younger boy learns to push beyond the limitations of his handicap. (Grades K-8)

The Olden Days Coat. Sal, a friendly, adventurous girl of ten, is disappointed that she and her parents will spend the Christmas holidays at her grandmother's country house instead of at home in the city as is their custom. Once there and in search of excitement, Sal explores the attic of the house. She finds a coat in a trunk and goes back in time. She meets Gran as a young girl. A special gift affords Sal and her grandmother an opportunity to express their love for one another and share warm feelings of the holidays and of understanding. (Grades 6-8)

The Tap Dance Kid. Eight-year-old Willie tap dances through his days dreaming of performing on Broadway. His uncle, a dance pro, encourages him but is strongly opposed by Willie's father. Willie's twelve-year-old sister, who wants to become a lawyer, is the only one willing to help him attain his goal, so she takes on Willie as a perfect "test case." (Grades 4-8)

The Ugly Little Boy. This is a science fiction movie. A Neanderthal boy is brought into the present time to be studied. A nurse who has no family, no friends, and no emotional involvements is selected to care for him during the two hundred days he is to be studied.

What transpires between the nurse and the boy is the thrust of this film. Can feelings and emotions be left out? There is a surprise ending. (Grades 6-8)

Tillie, the Unhappy Hippopotamus. An animated tale of a little hippo who lives on the river. Usually quite happy, Tillie loses faith in herself when she overhears a man describe hippos as "ugly, thick-skinned grunters." Ashamed of herself and what she is, Tillie rushes to the magic flower, wishing to be changed. Through her experiences as a butterfly, a fish, and a bird, Tillie learns that happiness comes from within, and that being a hippo is as wonderful as being anything at all. (Grades K-5)

Very Special Friends. Two sisters have a very special relationship. Then the younger sister falls out of their tree house and dies. The older sister has to work through her grief. (Grades 6-8)

Why We Need Each Other: Animals' Picnic Day. One person is often very different from another, and this story introduces the concept that those differences can be beneficial to all of us. (Grades K-3)

Disney Educational Productions
Distributed by Coronet/MTI Film & Video
108 Wilmot Road
Deerfield, Illinois 60015
(The following are color filmstrips and cassette programs.)

Back to School with Winnie the Pooh. Classroom Citizenship with Tigger, Learning Skills with Eeyore, School Citizenship with Roo, Self-esteem with Winnie the Pooh, and Being New with Piglet. (Primary)

Winnie the Pooh and the Right Thing to Do. In Which Pooh Learns Not to Endanger Others, In Which Piglet Learns Not to Keep Lost Property, In Which Tigger Learns Not to Cheat, In Which Rabbit Learns Not to Steal, In Which Tigger Learns Not to Lie, In Which Roo Learns Not to Destroy Property. (Primary)

Teenage Stress: Before It's Too Late (teenage suicide); *A Time to Tell* (sexual abuse) (Junior/Senior High)

Family Problems: Dealing with Crisis. Looking at Death, Grieving, When Parents Separate, After the Divorce, When Families Move, The New Neighborhood. (Junior/ Senior High)

FilmFair Communications
10621 Magnolia Blvd.
North Hollywood, California 91601

The Day My Kid Went Punk. To his parents, Terry Warner is a source of pride, but Terry feels ignored at home, and by girls as well. In order to conform he goes "punk," to the dismay of his parents. If he is the same person inside, why can't his parents see that and not worry about the way he dresses? The story emphasizes the need for communication between people . . . parents and teenagers. (Junior/Senior High)

There's Nobody Else Like You. Children learn from this film that they are unique, and that both differences and similarities between people can be enjoyed. These elements are revealed in a class trip to the zoo and during recess on the school playground. (Primary/ Elementary)

One More Hurdle. Challenged by the negative comment of a playmate, seven-year-old Donna Marie Cheek boasted that she, too, could ride a horse and win contests. However, once astride a horse, her dream to win ribbons like those of her friend quickly gave way to a love of horses and the desire to be an equestrian. This true story is not only a testament to one woman's struggle to achieve, but also to the strength of a family united. It is a remarkable story of endurance and fulfillment of a dream. (Junior/Senior High)

Square Pegs, Round Holes. Based on the original story by Phyllis Harvey, this animated film begins with the birth of a cube. As it grows, it finds it doesn't like to chase cats like the other kids, it reads books while its parents watch TV, and all in all just isn't like its fellow shapes—the cones, the spheres, etc.—who easily fall into grooves made for them. He finally realizes they are all unique. He digs his own hole, jumps in, and eventually finds his own unique way of life. (Upper Elementary/Junior/Senior High)

That's Stealing. This is the story of two friends. They are middle-class children who have just about everything they need or want. One friend developed a bad habit. She started taking things that do not belong to her—stealing. The other friend chooses to "look the other way," accepting that "it's no big deal." However, one day, something of Kathy's is taken from her desk at school and she is forced to deal with her friend and the issue between them. (Primary/Elementary)

Gossip. Jenny's friend Amy is spreading gossip about a girl at school. Jenny feels it's not right, but Amy tells her that "a little gossip never hurt anybody." Unfortunately, because of the gossip, the innocent victim, Terri, is being shunned by her classmates. Jenny feels she must do something to help stop the gossip. She seeks advice from her tutor, who gives her some ways of dealing with gossip. Jenny is still torn between her friendship with Amy and her own sense of what is right, until one day things get out of hand at school and she has to decide what to do. (Elementary/Junior High)

Teamwork. This animated film illustrates the benefits of people working and cooperating with each other. The entertaining story centers on monks and how they eventually learn to work together on the task of replenishingthe water supply. A fire in the temple forces the monks to desperately work together. Through their newfound cooperation and teamwork they find the solution to their problems. (Elementary/Junior /Senior High)

National Education Association
1201 16th Street, N.W.
Washington, D.C. 20036

A Desk for Billie. The first memories of Billie's childhood were of dusty roads, an open car, a tent pitched for sleeping. She had no real home. She felt her family was not real, not like people who live in houses. She asked how one became "real people" and what made the children in the town different from her. A hobo gave her the answer. School, he explained. "Real children" went to school, and the schools were free! So Billie started to school, and her life changed—thanks to kind and understanding teachers. The audience will pull for Billie as she overcomes many obstacles to receive an education. This film is extremely motivational for students. (Grades 4-8) (Teachers, Parents)

Phoenix Films & Video
468 Park Avenue South
New York, New York 10016

Annie and the Old One. This is the story of a Navajo girl named Annie who loves to hear the stories her grandmother, the Old One, tells. One day the Old One reveals a sad truth—when the new rug on the loom is finished, she will go to Mother Earth. Sadness comes to Annie. She cannot imagine life without her and plots to keep the rug from completion. The Old One discovers Annie's distress and helps her to understand the cycle of life. (Grades 5-8)

Dr. Seuss on the Loose. Pressure to conform, inevitability of change, resistance to try something new form the basis of the madcap adventures of the creative mind of Dr. Seuss. Three stories are combined: "The Sneetches," "The Zax," and "Green Eggs and Ham." (Grades 1-8)

Mandy's Grandmother. Mandy's grandmother is coming for a visit. She has never met her before, but she has a picture book with a grandmother in the story, and that has given her an idea of what her grandmother should be like. But when her grandmother arrives, it isn't as she had imagined it would be. Film tells the story of how Mandy and her grandmother begin to love and accept each other for who they are. (Grades 5-8)

My Turtle Died Today. A boy recalls the death of a pet. Efforts to help his sick turtle fail, and the boy and his friends bury it and question one another about some of the realities of death. They discover a pet cat has given birth to a litter of kittens, which creates discussion on the inevitability of death and the continuity of life. (Grades 1-6)

They Call Me Names. A documentary film portraying the lives of mentally different young people and how they perceive a world in which they are told often and in many ways that they are retarded. Viewers are made aware of the sensitivity to their own problems, and to the pain experienced almost daily by young people who must live with this stereotype. (Grades 6-8)

Pyramid Films
P. O. Box 1048
Santa Monica, California 90406-1408

Are People All the Same? Clarifies the term "human"; defines the word "race"; examines the assumption that all strangers of other races look alike. Japanese and Chinese children stand side by side and the point is made that there is something special about everyone we get to know. Visuals celebrate the uniqueness of each and every person. (Grades K-4)

Get It Together. Jeff Minnebraker was a college student when he was involved in an automobile accident that left him paralyzed from the waist down. Since the accident, he has married, returned to college, and become a recreational therapist for other handicapped individuals. Scenes show Jeff's interaction with his patients, his relationship with his wife, and how his independent spirit contributes to human potential knowledge. (Grades 6-8)

Oh Brother, My Brother. Focusing on the love and affection two young brothers feel for each other, film follows the boys' activities from morning to evening. It captures the normal conflicts of early childhood while showing these conflicts within the framework of the joy that the boys find in each other's presence. (Grades 1-8)

The Truth about Teachers. A wonderful video to share with faculties. It reminds us of why we went into teaching—to make it good for them, the students. (Teachers, Parents)

NOTE: All of the above companies are excellent sources for films/videos in the area of self-esteem. This is only a partial listing of the films/videos available from these companies. Check with your audio-visual department and look over their catalogs for many other films/videos that will enhance your study of self in the classroom.

13
EVALUATION

Although I used the Piers-Harris Children's Self-Concept Scale for pre- and post testing with my fourth-graders in those beginning years, I have been somewhat reluctant to overemphasize the testing aspect with my teacher-students. I have a concern with "pencil and papering" students in the subject of self-esteem, and tend to trust my own instincts on this issue. However, some may feel that testing is the only way to evalute gain; this must be left to the individual teacher. In my observation, children appear happier, most confident, and willing to take risks, are more open to sharing, and show improvement in academic subjects as a result of the emphasis on building self-esteem in the classroom. Test results may play a role in evaluating their progress; however, one's own sense of what is happening with these children throughout the program should be given equal weight. With this caveat in mind, I offer the following tests that are available. Obviously anything that will assist us in gaining insight in this area is worth considering.

I would like to refer you to *Taxonomy of Educational Objectives—The Classification of Educational Goals, Handbook II: Affective Domain,* by David R. Krathwohl, Benjamin S. Bloom, and Bertram B. Masia, David McKay Company, Inc., 1964. This book will help you in determining and writing behavorial objectives in the affective domain. The authors, at the beginning of the book, share some of their frustrations of writing objectives and evaluating in the affective domain. However, I found this book very helpful. Perhaps you will, too.

In the last pages of his book *The Antecedents of Self-Esteem,* Dr. Stanley Coopersmith developed a self-esteem inventory for students, teachers, and parents. Dr. Michele Borba, in the appendix of her book *Esteem Builders,* offers a self-esteem tally to assess students in five esteem components, i.e., security, selfhood, affiliation, mission, and competence.

The following are listed as resources for your information:

Consulting Psychologists Press, Inc.
577 College Avenue
Palo Alto, California 94306

Behavioral Academic Self-Esteem (B), by Stanley Coopersmith and Ragnar Gilberts (BASE) is an observational rating scale that assesses the academic self-esteem of children preschool (age 4) through grade 8 (age 14). It can be completed by a teacher, parent, or professional with access to sustained direct observation of the child. BASE assesses student initiative, social attention, success/failure, social attraction, and self-confidence.

Coopersmith Self-Esteem Inventory

This test was designed to measure general self-esteem and five other subcategories of self-esteem in children ages 8-15 and 16 and older. Subscales include the following: social self-peers, home-parents, school-academic, total self, lie scale score.

National Center for Effective Schools
1025 W. Johnson Street
Madison, Wisconsin 53706

Wisconsin Youth Survey

This test was designed and used over a five-year period to evaluate secondary programs for at-risk youth. It measures the following domains: sociocentric reasoning; social bonding to peers, schools, teachers; academic self-concept; negative teacher behavior; perception of opportunity; conventional roles; locus on control; self-esteem.

Publishers Test Service
2500 Garden Road
Del Monte Research Park
Monterey, California 93940

The following are tests available from this company:
The Culture-Free Self-Esteem Inventories for Children and Adults
Self-Concept Scale for Children (Grades 2+)

Science Research Associates, Inc.
155 N. Wacker Drive
Chicago, Illinois 60606

Minnesota School Attitude Survey

This test assesses attitudes toward school for both elementary and secondary levels. The survey includes the following clusters: feelings about academic subjects, school personnel, peers, self-expression, learning situations, themselves, and the school setting. Two forms are available, one for grades 1-3 and one for grades 4-12.

Drs. George Spivack and Marshall Swift
Dept. of Mental Health Sciences
Hahnemann University
1505 Race Street
Philadelphia, Pennsylvania 19102

Hahnemann Behavior Rating Scale

This test is available for both the elementary (HESB) and high school (HHSB) levels. Teachers rate students' behaviors in these areas: originality, independent learning, involvement, productivity with peers, intellectual dependency with peers, failure anxiety, unreflectiveness, irrelevant talk, disruptive social involvement, negative feelings, holding back/withdrawn, critical-competitive, blaming approach to teaching, inattention, academic achievement.

Western Psychological Services
12031 Wilshire Blvd.
Los Angeles, California 90025

The Piers-Harris Children's Self-Concept Scale

This test was designed for use with children in grades 4-12 to measure total self-concept in six clusters: behavior, intellectual and school status, physical appearance and attributes, anxiety, popularity, and happiness and satisfaction.

14
SUGGESTED READING
FOR CHILDREN

Amoss, Berthe. *Tom in the Middle.* Harper & Row, 1968.

Ancona, George. *I Feel: A Picture Book of Emotions.* Dutton, 1977.

Arkhurst, Joyce Cooper. *The Adventures of Spider* (retold). Little, Brown & Co., 1964.

Armstrong, William H. *Sounder.* Harper & Row, 1969.

Asheron, Sara. *How to Find a Friend.* Grosset & Dunlap, 1964.

Austin, Lou. *The Little Me and the Great Me.* Partnership Foundation, 1957.

Bailey, Carolyn Sherwin. *The Little Rabbit Who Wanted Red Wings.* Platt & Munk, 1961.

Barkin, Carol. *Are We Still Friends?* Raintree, 1975.

_____. *Doing Things Together.* Raintree, 1975.

_____. *I'd Rather Stay Home.* Raintree, 1975.

_____. *Sometimes I Hate School.* Raintree, 1975.

Baylor, Byrd. *Amigo.* Macmillan, 1963.

Behrens, June. *How I Feel.* Childrens Press, 1973.

_____. *Together.* Childrens Press, 1975.

Beim, Jerrold. *The Smallest Boy in the Class.* Morrow, 1949.

Bel Geddes, Barbara. *I Like to Be Me.* Viking Press, 1963.

Berger, Terry. *Being Alone, Being Together.* Advanced Learning Concepts, 1974.

_____. *Big Sister, Little Brother.* Advanced Learning Concepts, 1974.

_____. *A Friend Can Help.* Advanced Learning Concepts, 1974.

_____. *How Does It Feel When Your Parents Get Divorced?* Messner, 1977.

_____. *I Have Feelings* Behavioral Publications, 1971.

_____. *A New Baby.* Advanced Learning Concepts, 1974.

Bishop, Curtis. *Little League Victory.* Lippincott, 1967.

Bishop, Claire. *The Five Chinese Brothers.* Coward-McCann, 1938.

Blood, Charles L., and Martin Link. *The Goat in the Rug.* Macmillan Publishing Company, 1976.

Blume, Judy. *Are You There God? It's Me, Margaret.* Bradbury, 1970.

_____. *Blubber.* Bradbury, 1974.

_____. *Beanie.* Bradbury, 1973.

_____. *It's Not the End of the World.* Bradbury, 1972.

_____. *Otherwise Known as Sheila the Great.* Button, 1972.

_____. *Tales of a Fourth-Grade Nothing.* Button, 1972.

Bonsall, Crosby. *The Case of the Cat's Meow.* Harper & Row, 1965.

_____. *The Case of the Hungry Stranger.* Harper & Row, 1963.

_____. *The Case of the Scaredy Cats.* Harper & Row, 1971.

Boone, Debby. *Bedtime Hugs for Little Ones.* Harvest House Publishers, 1988.

Bradbury, Peggy. *The Snake That Couldn't Slither.* Putnam, 1976.

Bragdon, Elspeth. *That Jod!* Viking Press, 1962.

Brandenberg, Aliki. *Feelings.* Mulberry Books/Wm. Morrow & Co., 1984.

Brown, Marcia. *Stone Soup: An Old Tale.* Scribner, 1947.

Brown, Margaret Wise. *The Important Book.* Harper & Row, 1949.

Burnett, Frances Hodgson. *The Secret Garden.* Dell, 1911.

Burnford, Sheila. *The Incredible Journey.* Bantam, 1960.

Buscaglia, Leo. *The Fall of Freddie Leaf.* Charles B. Slack, Inc., 1982.

Butters, Dorothy Gilman. *The Bells of Freedom.* Macrae Smith Company, 1963.

Byers, Betsy. *The Summer of the Swans.* Avon/Camelot, 1970.

Carlsen, Ruth Christopher. *Henrietta Goes West.* Houghton, 1966.

Caudill, Rebecca. *A Certain Small Shepard.* Holt, Rinehart and Winston, 1965.

_____. *Did You Carry the Flag Today, Charley?* Holt, Rinehart and Winston, 1966.

Clifton, Lucille. *Everett Anderson's Good-bye.* Henry Holt & Company,1983.

Cohen, Miriam. *Best Friends.* Macmillan, 1971.

_____. *Lost in the Museum.* Greenwillow, 1979.

_____. *The New Teacher.* Macmillan, 1972.

_____. *Tough Jim.* Macmillan, 1974.

_____. *When Will I Read?* Greenwillow, 1977.

_____. *Will I Have a Friend?* Macmillan, 1967.

Colman, Hila. *Nobody Has to Be a Kid Forever.* Crown, 1976.

Conta, Marcia Maher. *Feelings Between Friends.* Advanced Learning Concepts, 1974.

Cosgrove, Stephen. Serendipity Books

_____. *In Search of the Saveopotomas.*

_____. *The Muffin Muncher.*

_____. *Serendipity.*

_____. *Jack O'Shawnasey.*

_____. *Morgan and Me.*

_____. *Flutterby.*

_____. *Nitter Pitter.*

_____. *Leo the Lop.*

_____. *Tail Two.*

_____. *Kartusch.*

_____. *The Gnome from Nome.*

_____. *The Wheedle on the Needle.*

_____. *The Dream Tree.*

_____. *Hucklebug.*

_____. *Creole.*

_____. *Bangalee.*

_____. *Catundra.*

_____. *Cap'n Smudge.*

_____. *Maui-Maui.*

_____. *Little Mouse on the Prairie.* Price/Stern/Sloan Publishers, Inc., 410 North La Cienega Boulevard, Los Angeles, California 90048.

Dahl, Roald. *Charlie and the Chocolate Factory.* Bantam, 1964.

_____. *James and the Giant Peach.* Knopf, 1961.

Dansinger, Paula. *The Cat Ate My Gymsuit.* Delacorta, 1974.

_____. *The Pistachio Prescription.* Delacorta, 1978.

dePaola, Tommie. *Nana Upstairs & Nana Downstairs.* G. P. Putnam's, 1973.

Edwards, Julie. *Mandy.* Bantam, 1971.

Elkin, Benjamin. *Lucky and the Giant.* Childrens Press, 1962.

Emberley, Ed. *The Great Thumbprint Drawing Book.* Little, Brown & Co., 1977.

Estes, Eleanor. *The Hundred Dresses.* Scholastic, 1972.

Evans, Eva Knox. *All About Me.* Golden Press, 1947.

_____. *People Are Important.* Golden Press, 1951.

Evans, Katherine. *The Boy Who Cried Wolf* (retold). Albert Whitman, 1979.

_____. *The Man, the Boy and the Donkey.* Albert Whitman, 1958.

Fassler, Joan. *Don't Worry, Dear.* Behavioral Publications, 1971.

_____. *Howie Finds Himself.* Whitman, 1975.

_____. *The Man of the House.* Behavioral Publications, 1969.

_____. *One Little Girl.* Behavioral Publications, 1969.

Foote, Patricia. *Girls Can Be Anything They Want.* Messner, 1980.

Fox, Mim. *Wilfred, Gordon, McDonald, Partridge.* Kane Miller Publishing, 1985.

Freeman, Don. *Corduroy.* Penguin Books, 1968.

Friskey, Margaret. *Rackety, That Very Special Rabbit.* Childrens Press, 1965.

Gag, Wanda. *Millions of Cats.* Coward-McCann & Geoghegan, 1928.

Gates, Doris. *Blue Willow.* Viking, 1940.

Gay, Kathlyn. *Family Is For Living: The Changing Family in a Changing World.* Delacorte Press, 1972.

Gelfend, Ravina. *They Wouldn't Quit: Stories of Handicapped People.* Lerner Publications, 1962.

George, Jean. *My Side of the Mountain.* E. P. Dutton, 1959.

Greenfield, Eloise. *Tosa Park.* Thomas Y. Crowell, 1973.

Grimm, Jakob Ludwig Karl (Brothers Grimm). *Shoemaker and Elves.* Scribner, 1960.

Guideposts. *Champions. What Made Them Great?* Guideposts, Carmel, New York 10512.

Guilfoile, Elizabeth. *Nobody Listens to Andrew.* Follett, 1957.

Hall, Brian. *Nog's Vision*. Paulist Press, 1973.

Hamilton, Morse. *My Name Is Emily*. Greenwillow, 1979.

Heide, Florence Parry. *When the Sad One Comes to Stay*. Bantam Books, 1975.

Hints, Sandy. *We Can't Afford It*. Raintree, 1977.

Hoban, Russell. *The Little Brute Family*. Avon, 1966.

_____. *The Stone Doll of Sister Brute*. Avon, 1968.

Hoff, Syd. *Irving & Me*. Dell, 1967.

Holland, Isabelle. *Dinah and the Green Fat Kingdom*. Lippincott, 1978.

Johnson, Spencer. Value Tales Series. Using famous people in history, Dr. Johnson teaches lessons in understanding, helping, fantasy, friendship, curiosity, courage, caring, truth, trust, humor, kindness, believing in yourself, sharing, determination, patience, honesty, love, dedication, foresight, saving, fairness, imagination, respect, giving, learning and responsibility. (25+ books) Value Communications, Inc., Publishers, LaJolla, California 92038.

Kahl, Virginia. *Maxie*. Scribner, 1956.

Kalb, Johan. *What Every Kid Should Know*. Houghton, 1976.

Keats, Ezra Jack. *Goggles*. Macmillan, 1970.

_____. *The Little Drummer Boy*. Harper, 1968.

_____. *Peter's Chair*. Harper, 1967.

Kennedy, John F. *Profiles in Courage*. Harper & Row, 1961.

Kennedy, Richard. *Come Again in the Spring*. Harper & Row, 1976.

_____. *The Parrot and the Thief*. Little, Brown & Co., 1974.

Kesler, Jay, with Tim Stafford. *I Never Promised You a Disneyland*. Word Books, 1975.

Konigsburg, E. L. *From the Mixed Up Files of Mrs. Basil E. Frankweiler*. Dell, 1967.

Kraus, Robert. *Boris Bad Enough*. Windmill Books/Dutton, 1976.

_____. *Leo the Latebloomer*. Windmill Books/Dutton, 1971.

_____. *Owliver*. Windmill Books/Dutton, 1974.

Krauss, Ruth. *The Growing Story*. Harper & Row, 1947.

Kroll, Steven. *That Makes Me Mad*. Pantheon, 1976.

Lamorisse, Albert. *The Red Balloon*. Doubleday, 1956.

Leaf, Munro. *The Story of Ferdinand*. Viking, 1938.

LeShan, Eda J. *Learning to Say Good-bye*. Macmillan, 1976.

_____. *What's Going to Happen to Me?* Four Winds, 1978.

_____. *What Makes Me Feel This Way?* Macmillan, 1972.

_____. *You and Your Feelings*. Macmillan, 1975.

Lessor, Richard. *Fuzzies, a Folk Fable*. Argus Communications, 1971.

Lionni, Leo. *Frederick*. Pantheon, 1967.

_____. *Fezzettino*. Pantheon, 1975.

_____. *Swimmy*. Pantheon, 1963.

_____. *Tico and the Golden Wings*. Pantheon, 1964.

Lipkind, William, and Nicolas Mardvinoff. *Finders Keepers*. Harcourt, Brace & World, 1951.

Lobel, Anita. *The Troll Music*. Harper & Row, 1966.

McCloskey, Robert. *Make Way for Ducklings*. Viking Press, 1941.

McDermott, Gerald. *Anansi the Spider*. Holt, Rinehart & Winston, 1975.

McGovern, Ann. *Stone Soup*. Scholastic, 1968.

Mack, Nancy. *I'm Not Going*. Raintree, 1976.

————. *Tracy*. Raintree, 1976.

————. *Why Me?* Raintree, 1976.

Madison, Winifred. *Call Me Danica*. Four Winds, 1977.

Mann, Peggy. *There Are Two Kinds of Terrible*. Doubleday, 1977.

Marshall, James. *Miss Nelson Is Missing*. Scholastic, 1977.

Mayer, Mercer. *There's a Nightmare in My Closet*. Dial Press, 1968.

Merrill, Jean. *The Toothpaste Millionaire*. Houghton Mifflin, 1972.

Miles, Betty. *Just the Beginning*. Knopf, 1976.

————. *The Real Me*. Avon, 1974.

Muller, Romeo. *Puff the Magic Dragon*. Avon, 1979.

Mueller, Charles S. and Donald R. Bardill. *Thank God I'm a Teenager*. Augsburg
    Publishing House, 1976.

Munsch, Robert. *Love You Forever*. Firefly Books, Ltd., 1986.

Nardine, Elisabeth. *Daydreams and Nightmares*. Raintree, 1976.

Nathan, Dorothy. *Women of Courage*. Random House, 1964.

O'Dell, Scott. *Island of the Blue Dolphins*. Dell, 1960.

Odor, Ruth. *Cissy, the Pup*. Child's World, 1976.

————. *Lori's Day*. Child's World, 1976.

————. *Sarah Lou's Untied Shoes*. Child's World, 1976.

Pappas, Michael G. *Sweet Dreams for Little Ones—Bedtime Fantasies to Build Self-
    Esteem*. Harper & Row, 1982.

Patterson, A. B. *Waltzing Matilda*. Holt, Rinehart & Winston, 1970.

Paulus, Trina. *Hope for the Flowers*. Paulist Press, 1972.

Peck, Robert Newton. *A Day No Pigs Would Die*. Dell Publishing Co., 1972.

Peet, Bill. *How Droofus the Dragon Lost His Head*. Houghton Mifflin, 1971.

————. *Randy's Dandy Lions*. Houghton Mifflin, 1964.

————. *The Wump World*. Houghton Mifflin, 1979.

————. *Smokey*. Houghton Mifflin, 1962.

Pfeffer, Susan Beth. *Kid Power*. Watts, 1977.

Piper, Watty. *The Little Engine That Could*. Platt & Munk, 1930.

Porter, Gene Stratton. *Freckles*. Grosset, 1904.

————. *Girl of Limberlost*. Grosset, 1909.

Preston, Edna Mitchell. *The Temper Tantrum Book*. Penguin Books, 1969.

Raskin, Ellen. *Nothing Ever Happens on My Block*. Antheneum, 1971.

Rawlings, Marjorie Kinnan. *The Yearling*. Scribner's, 1939.

Rawls, Wilson. *Where the Red Fern Grows*. Bantam Books, 1961.

Rosenbaum, Jean. *What Is Fear?* Prentice-Hall, 1972.

Saint-Exupéry, Antoine de. *The Little Prince.* Harcourt, Brace & World, 1943.

Schlein, Meriam. *The Elephant Herd.* Junior Literary Guild, 1956.

Seeger, Pete, and Charles Seeger. *The Foolish Frog.* Macmillan, 1955.

Seixas, Judith S. *Living with a Parent Who Drinks Too Much.* Greenwillow Books, 1979.

Seldon, George. *The Cricket in Times Square.* Dell, 1960.

Sendak, Maurice. *Pierre.* Harper & Row, 1962.

Seuss, Dr. *Did I Ever Tell You How Lucky You Are?* Random House, 1973.

Sharmat, Marjorie Weinman. *A Big Fat Enormous Lie.* Dutton, 1978.

_____. *Gladys Told Me To Meet Her Here.* Harper & Row, 1970.

_____. *I Don't Care.* Macmillan, 1977.

_____. *I'm Not Oscar's Friend Anymore.* Dutton, 1975.

_____. *I'm Terrific.* Holiday House, 1976.

_____. *Mitchell Is Moving.* Macmillan, 1978.

_____. *Say Hello, Vanessa.* Holiday House, 1979.

Shedd, Charlie W. *Letters to Karen.* Abingdon, 1965.

_____. *Letters to Phillip.* Pyramid Books, 1968.

_____. *You Are Somebody Special.* McGraw-Hill, 1978.

Silverstein, Shel. *The Giving Tree.* Harper & Row, 1964.

_____. *The Missing Piece.* Harper & Row, 1976.

Simon, Norma. *How Do I Feel?* Albert Whitman, 1970.

_____. *I Know What I Like.* Albert Whitman, 1971.

_____. *I Was So Mad.* Albert Whitman, 1974.

_____. *What Do I Do?* Albert Whitman, 1969.

Sparks, Asa H. *Hope for the Frogs.* Jalmar, 1979.

Sperry, Armstrong. *Call It Courage.* Macmillan, 1940.

Stanton, Elizabeth. *Sometimes I Like to Cry.* Albert Whitman, 1978.

Sterling, Dorothy. *Mary Jane.* Doubleday, 1959.

Stevenson, James. *The Worst Person in the World.* Greenwillow, 1978.

Stuart, Jesse. *The Beatinest Boy.* McGraw-Hill, 1953.

_____. *A Penny's Worth of Character.* McGraw-Hill, 1956.

Sullivan, Mary Beth. *Feeling Free.* Addison-Wesley, 1979.

Tester, Sylvia Root. *Feeling Angry.* Child's World, 1976.

_____. *Sometimes I'm Afraid.* Child's World, 1979.

_____. *That Big Bruno.* Child's World, 1976.

Thomas, Marlo. *Free to Be . . . You and Me.* McGraw, 1974.

Thompson, Elaine. *Sparky, a Book about Feelings.* Durfee Press, 1977.

Udry, Janice May. *Let's Be Enemies.* School Book Service, 1969.

_____. *Now I Fade Away.* Albert Whitman, 1976.

_____. *What Mary Jo Shared.* Albert Whitman, 1966.

Viorst, Judith. *Alexander and the Terrible, Horrible, No Good, Very Bad Day.* Antheneum, 1973.

_____. *My Mama Says There Aren't Any Zombies, Ghosts, Vampires, Creatures, Demons, Monsters, Fiends, Goblins, or Things*. Antheneum, 1973.

_____. *The Tenth Good Thing About Barney*. Antheneum, 1971.

Wagner, Jane. *J.T.* Van Nostrand Peinhold, 1969.

Watson, Jane Werner. *Sometimes I Get Angry*. Golden Press, 1971.

Webster, Alice Jean. *Daddy-Long-Legs*. Grosset, 1912.

Weedn, Flavia. *Flavia and the Dream Maker*. Innocent Age Ltd., 1988.

White, E. B. *Charlotte's Web*. Harper & Row, 1952.

_____. *Stuart Little*. Harper & Row, 1945.

_____. *The Trumpet of the Swan*. Harper & Row, 1970.

William, Barbara. *Someday, Said William*. Dutton, 1976.

Williams, Margery. *The Velveteen Rabbit*. Doubleday, 1958.

Wolf, Bernard. *Adam Smith Goes to School*. Lippincott, 1978.

Wolitzer, Hilma. *Toby Lived Here*. Farrar, 1978.

Yates, Elizabeth. *Skeezer: A Dog with a Mission*. Harvey House, Inc., 1973.

Yep, Laurence. *Dragonwings*. Harper, 1975.

Zemach, Harve. *The Judge*. Farrar, Straus & Giroux, 1969.

_____. *The Tricks of Master Dabble*. Holt, Rinehart & Winston, 1965.

Zerafa. Judy. *Go for It!* Workman Publishing, 1986.

Ziegler, Sandra. *Something for Sara*. Child's World, 1977.

Ziglar, Zig. *See You at the Top*. Pelican Publishing Company, 1977.

Zolotow, Charlotte. *It's Not Fair*. Harper, 1976.

_____. *The New Friend*. Harper & Row, 1981.

_____. *The Quarreling Book*. Harper, 1963.

_____. *A Tiger Called Thomas*. Lothrop, 1963.

_____. *William's Doll*. Harper & Row, 1972.

ADDITIONAL RESOURCES

Brett, Doris. *Annie Stories—A Special Kind of Storytelling*. Workman Publishing, 1986.

Each chapter has a different problem Annie is dealing with in her life. As the teacher reads each story the class can discuss Annie's problem. This book provides for a safe, nonthreatening approach for children to discuss problems, which may also be problems in their lives. As they work through problems and solutions with Annie, they can also see implications for their lives. Recommended for preschool through intermediate grades.

Dreyer, Sharon Spredemann. *The Bookfinder—When Kids Need Books*. American Guidance Service.

This is a wonderful resource to lead teachers and children to books that deal with feelings and emotions. These books help children cope with the challenges in life. Through bibliotherapy (the use of reading materials to help solve emotional problems and to promote mental health) children learn that they are not the only ones dealing with life problems. They can safely identify with a story character, work through problems vicariously, and gain more insight into themselves and others. *The Bookfinder* has a very helpful introduction on how to use books to help children, complete with some research and information on bibliotherapy. There is a synopsis given of each book with suggested grade level. The books cover preschool through high school.

    K7550 Volume 1 (books through 1974) $54.95
    K7560 Volume 2 (books through 1975-1978) $54.95
    K7570 Volume 3 (books from 1979-1982) $64.95
    K758 1 Volume 4 (books from 1983-1986) $69.95
    K7580 Softcover set (v. 3-4) $59.00
    K7571 Volume 3, softcover $29.95
    K7582 Volume 4, softcover $34.95

American Guidance Service
Publishers Building
P. O. Box 99
Circle Pines, Minnesota 55014-1796
1-800-328-2560   In Minnesota, call 1-800-247-5053

Fassler, Joan. *Helping Children Cope* (Mastering Stress through Books and Stories). The Free Press/Division of Macmillan Publishing Company, Inc., 1978. (This is also a good resource for bibliotheraphy.)

15

SUGGESTED READING FOR ADULTS

Allen, Charles L. *God's Psychiatry*. Pyramid Books, 1953.

Allen, James. *As a Man Thinketh*. The Peter Piper Press, 1976.

Allport, G. W. *Becoming*. Yale University Press, 1955.

_____. *The Person in Psychology*. Beacon Press, 1958.

Anderson, Walter. *Courage Is a Three-Letter Word*. Ballatine Books, 1986.

_____. *The Greatest Risk of All*. Houghton Mifflin Company, 1988.

Ashby, W. Ross. *Cybernetics*. Chapman and Hall Ltd., 1958.

Ashton-Warner, Sylvia. *Teacher*. Bantam Books, 1963.

Aurandt, Paul. *Paul Harvey's the Rest of the Story*. Bantam Books, 1977.

Axline, Virginia. *Dibs, in Search of Self*. Ballantine Books, 1964.

Bach, Richard. *Illusions*. Delacorte Press, 1977.

_____. *Jonathan Livingston Seagull*. Avon, 1970.

Barksdale, L. S. *Building Self-Esteem*. The Barksdale Foundation, 1972.

Baucom, John Q. *Fatal Choice: The Teenage Suicide Crisis*. Moody Press, 1986.

Beattie, Melody. *Codependent No More—How to Stop Controlling Others and Start Caring for Yourself*. Harper & Row, 1987.

_____. *Beyond Codependence and Getting Better All the Time*. Harper & Row, 1989.

Beck, Joan. *Effective Parenting*. Simon and Schuster, 1976.

Beesing, Maria, Robert J. Nogosek, and Patrick H. O'Leary. *The Enneagram: A Journey of Self-Discovery*. Dimension Books, Inc., 1984.

Bettelheim, Bruno. *Love Is Not Enough*. Avon, 1950.

Bloom, Benjamin Samuel. *All Our Children Learning*. McGraw-Hill, 1981.

Bois, J. Samuel. *Explorations in Awareness*. Harper & Brothers, 1957.

Bradshaw, John. *Healing the Shame That Binds You*. Health Communications, Inc., 1988.

Bradshaw, Pete. *The Management of Self-Esteem*. Prentice-Hall, Inc., 1981.

Brandon, Nathaniel. *The Psychology of Self-Esteem*. Nash Publishing, 1969.

Brazelton, T. Berry. *Working and Caring.* Addison-Wesley Publishing Company, Inc., 1987.

Briggs, Dorothy. *Your Child's Self-Esteem.* Doubleday, 1970.

_____. *Celebrate Your Self.* Doubleday, 1977.

Bristol, Claude M. *The Magic of Believing.* Prentice-Hall, Inc., 1948.

_____. *TNT: The Power Within You.* Prentice-Hall, Inc., 1956.

Brookover, Wilbur, and others. *Elementary School Climate and School Achievement—A Brief Report.* College of Education, Michigan State University, East Lansing, Michigan, May, 1976.

Brookover, Wilbur. *School of Social Systems and Student Achievement.* Praeger, 1979.

Burns, Maureen A. *Run with Your Dreams.* Empey Enterprises, 810 Alexander Street, Greenville, Michigan 48838, 1982.

Buscaglia, Leo. *Love.* Slack Publishing, 1973.

Campbell, David. *If You Don't Know Where You're Going You'll Probably End Up Somewhere Else.* Argus Communications, 1974.

Clark, Aminah, Harris, Clemes, and Reynold Bean. *How To Raise Your Teenager's Self-Esteem.* Price/Stern/Sloan Publisher, Inc., 1978.

Clarke, Jean Illsley. *Self-Esteem: A Family Affair.* Winston Press, 1978.

Clarke, Jean Illsley. *Self-Esteem: A Family Affair.* (Leader Guide). Harper & Row, 1981.

Clemes, Harris, and Reynold Bean. *How to Raise Children's Self-Esteem.* Price/Stern/ Sloan Publishers, Inc., 1980.

Combs, Arthur. *Perceiving, Behaving, Becoming. Yearbook of the Association for Supervision and Curriculum Development.* 1701 K Street, N.W., Washington, D. C. 20006, 1962.

Coopersmith, Stanley. *The Antecedents of Self-Esteem.* W. H. Freeman & Co., 1967.

Cullum, Albert. *The Geranium on the Window Sill Just Died But Teacher You Went Right On.* Harlin Quist, Inc., Belgium, 1971.

Danforth, William H. *I Dare You.* American Youth Foundation, 1972.

Dennison, George. *The Lives of Children.* Random House, 1969.

Dinkmeyer, Don, and Lewis E. Losoncy. *The Encouragement Book.* Prentice Hall Press, 1987.

Dobson, James C. *Dare to Discipline.* Tyndale House, 1970.

_____. *Hide or Seek.* Revell, 1974.

Drummond, Henry. *The Greatest Thing in the World.* Collins, London.

Dyer, Wayne W. *What Do You Really Want for Your Children?* William Morrow and Company, Inc., 1985.

_____. *You'll See It When You Believe It.* Morrow & Co., Inc., 1989.

_____. *Your Erroneous Zones*. Funk & Wagnalls, 1976.

Elkind, David. *The Hurried Child*. Addison-Wesley Publishing Company, 1981.

Fabun, Don. *Three Roads to Awareness*. Glencoe Press, 1979.

Feldman, Beverly. *Kids Who Succeed*. Ballantine Books, 1987.

Ford, Edward E., and Steven Englund. *For the Love of Children*. Anchor Press/ Doubleday, 1977.

Frankl, Viktor. *Man's Search for Meaning*. Washington Square Press, 1963.

_____. *The Unheard Cry for Meaning*. Simon and Schuster, 1979.

Frey, Diane, and C. Jesse Carlock. *Enhancing Self-Esteem*. Accelerated Development, Inc., 1984.

Fromm, Erich. *The Art of Loving*. Harper & Row, 1956.

Gardner, John. *No Easy Victories*. Harper & Row, 1968.

_____. *Self-Renewal*. Harper & Row, 1963.

Ginott, Haim G. *Between Parent and Child*. Macmillan, 1965.

_____. *Teacher and Child*. Macmillan, 1972.

Glasser, William. *Control Theory in the Classroom*. Harper & Row, 1986.

_____. *Positive Addiction*. Harper & Row, 1976.

_____. *Reality Therapy*. Harper & Row, 1965.

_____. *Schools Without Failure*. Harper & Row, 1969.

_____. *The Identity Society*. Harper & Row, 1975.

Goble, Frank. *The Third Force*. Grossman, 1979.

Goertzel, Victor, and Mildred. *Cradles of Eminence*. Little, Brown & Co., 1962.

Gordon, Thomas. *P.E.T., Parent Effectiveness Training*. Wyden, 1979.

_____. *T.E.T., Teacher Effectiveness Training*. Wyden, 1974.

Harris, Sydney J. *Winners and Losers*. Argus Communications, 1968.

Harris, Thomas A. *I'm OK—You're OK*. Funk and Wagnalls, 1967.

Hart, Louise. *The Winning Family: Increasing Self-Esteem in Children and Yourself*. LifeSkills Press, 1990.

Holt, John. *How Children Learn*. Dell, 1967.

Howe, Leland W., and Mary Martha. *Personalizing Education: Values Clarification and Beyond*. Hart Publishing Co., Inc., 1975.

Humphreys, Alice Lee. *Angels in Pinafores*. John Knox Press, 1967.

_____. *Heaven in My Hand*. John Knox Press, 1965.

Hyatt, Carole, and Linda Gottlieb. *When Smart People Fail—Rebuilding Yourself for Success*. Penguin Books, 1987.

James, Muriel. *Born to Love*. Addison-Wesley Publishing Company, 1973.

James, Muriel, and Dorothy Jongeward. *Born to Win*. Appleton Publishers, 1973.

James, William. *Principles of Psychology.* Dover, 1950.

Jampolsky, Gerald G. *Love Is Letting Go of Fear.* Bantam Books, 1979.

Johnson, David W. *Reaching Out: Interpersonal Effectiveness and Self-Actualization.* Prentice-Hall, Inc., 1972.

Joseph, Stephen M. *The Me Nobody Knows.* Avon, 1969.

Kennedy, Eugene. *If You Really Knew Me, Would You Still Like Me?* Argus, 1975.

Kerman, Sam. *Teacher Expectation and Student Acheivement Project.* Los Angeles County Schools, 9300 Imperial Highway, Downey, California 90242.

Kidder, Tracy. *Among School Children.* Houghton Mifflin, 1989.

Kinnear, W. H. Ed. *The Creative Power of Mind.* Prentice-Hall, 1957.

Kohlberg, Lawrence. *Collected Papers on Moral Development and Moral Education.* Moral Education and Research Foundation, 1975, Cambridge, Massachusetts (2 volumes).

Kopp, Sheldon B. *If You Meet the Buddha on the Road, Kill Him!* Bantam, 1972.

Kozol, Jonathan. *Death at an Early Age.* Houghton Mifflin Company, 1967.

Kübler-Ross, Elisabeth. *On Death and Dying.* Macmillan, 1969.

Lansky, Vicki. *101 Ways to Tell Your Child "I Love You."* Contemporary Books, Inc., 1988.

Leman, Kevin, and Randy Carlson. *Unlocking the Secrets of Your Childhood Memories.* Thomas Nelson Publishers, 1989.

Lecky, Prescott. *Self-Consistency: A Theory of Personality.* The Island Press, 1972.

Lembo, John. *Help Yourself.* Argus Communications, 1974.

Leonard, George B. *Education and Ecstasy.* Dell, 1968.

LeShan, Eda. *How to Survive Parenthood.* Random House, 1965.

_____. *In Search of Myself—and Other Children.* Lippincott, 1976.

_____. *Learning to Say Good-bye.* Avon Books, 1976.

_____. *The Conspiracy Against Childhood.* Antheneum, 1967.

_____. *Winning the Losing Battle.* Bantam Books, 1979.

Lessor, Richard. *Fuzzies, A Folk Fable.* Argus Communications, 1971.

Luft, J. *On Human Interaction.* National Press, 1969.

MacCracken, Mary. *Lovey: A Very Special Child.* Signet Books, 1976.

McKay, Matthew, and Patrick Fanning. *Self-Esteem.* St. Martin's Press, 1987.

Maltz, Maxwell. *Creative Living for Today.* Trident Press, 1967.

_____. *Psycho-Cybernetics.* Prentice-Hall, 1969.

_____. *Psycho-Cybernetic Principles for Creative Living.* Pocket Books, 1974.

_____. *The Magic Power of Self-Image Psychology.* Simon & Schuster, 1976.

Mandino, Og. *The Choice.* Bantam Books, Inc., 1984.

_____. *The Greatest Salesman in the World.* Frederick Fell, Inc., 1968.

Marshall, Catherine. *Beyond Ourselves.* Avon Books, 1961.

Maslow, Abraham H. *Motivation and Personality.* Harper & Row, 1954.

_____. *Toward a Psychology of Being.* Van Nostrand Company, Ltd., 1961.

Menninger, Karl. *Whatever Became of Sin?* Hawthorne Books, Inc., 1973.

Mitchell, William. *The Power of Positive Students.* William Morrow and Company, Inc., 1985.

Montague, Ashley. *On Being Human.* Henry Schuman, 1950.

Moustakas, Clarke E. *The Authentic Teacher: Sensitivity and Awareness in the Classroom.* Howard A. Doyle, 1966.

Moustakas, Clark E., and Cereta Perry. *Learning to Be Free.* Prentice-Hall, 1973.

Murphy, Gardner. *Human Potentialities.* Basic Books, 1958.

Murphy, Joseph. *The Power of the Subconscious Mind.* Prentice-Hall, 1963.

Newman, Robert E. *Reading, Writing, and Self-Esteem.* Spectrum Books. Prentice-Hall, 1982.

Olson, Ken. *The Art of Hanging Loose in an Uptight World.* Fawcett, 1974.

_____. *Can You Wait Until Friday?* O'Sullivan, Woodside & Company, 1974.

Overstreet, H. A. *The Mature Mind.* W. W. Norton & Co., Inc., 1949.

Paulus, Trina. *Hope for the Flowers.* Paulist Press, 1972.

Peairs, Lillian. *What Every Child Needs.* Harper & Row, 1974.

Peale, Norman Vincent. *Enthusiasm Makes the Difference.* Prentice-Hall, 1967.

_____. *The Power of Positive Thinking.* Prentice-Hall, 1952.

_____. *You Can If You Think You Can.* Prentice-Hall, 1974.

Peck, M. Scott. *The Road Less Traveled.* Simon and Schuster, 1978.

Perls, Frederick S., Ralph Hefferline, and Paul Goodman. *Gestalt Therapy.* Julian Press, 1958.

Peterson, Wilferd. *The Art of the Living Treasure Chest.* Simon and Schuster, 1977.

Postman, Neil. *The School Book.* Dell, 1975.

Powell, John. *Fully Human, Fully Alive.* Argus Communications, 1976.

_____. *The Secret of Staying in Love.* Argus Communications, 1974.

_____. *Why Am I Afraid to Love?* Argus Communications, 1972.

_____. *Why Am I Afraid to Tell You Who I Am?* Argus Communications, 1969.

Prescott, Daniel A. *Emotion and the Education Process.* American Council on Education, Washington, D. C., 1938.

Purkey, Sr., William W. *Self-Concept and School Acheivement.* Prentice-Hall, 1979.

Rainer, Tristine. *The New Diary* (Journal Writing). J. P. Tarcher, Inc., 1978.

Rath/Harmin/Simon. *Values and Teaching.* Charles E. Merrill Books, Inc., 1966.

Reid, Gavin. *A New Happiness.* Abingdon Press, 1974.

Robert, Marc. *Loneliness in the Schools.* Argus Communications, 1972.

_____. *School Morale.* Argus Communications, 1976.

Robertiello, Richard C. *Hold Them Very Close, Then Let Them Go.* Dial Press, 1975.

Rogers, Carl. *On Becoming a Person.* (Sentry Editions) Houghton, Mifflin Co., 1970.

_____. *On Personal Power.* Delta, 1977.

Rosenthal, Robert, and Lenore Jacobson. *Pygmalion in the Classroom.* Holt, Rinehart and Winston, 1968.

Rothman, Esther P. *The Angel Inside Went Sour.* Bantam Books, 1979.

Rubin, Theodore Isaac. *The Winner's Notebook.* Pocket Books, 1967.

Saint-Exupéry, Antoine de. *The Little Prince.* Harcourt, Brace and World, 1943.

Salk, Lee. *Preparing for Childhood.* David McKay, 1975.

Sanford, John A. *Healing and Wholeness.* Paulist Press, 1977.

Sanford, Linda Tschirhart, and Mary Ellen Donovan. *Women and Self-Esteem.* Penguin Books, 1984.

Satir, Virginia. *Peoplemaking.* Science and Behavior Books, Inc., 1972.

_____. *Self-Esteem.* Celestial Arts, 1979.

_____. *Your Many Faces.* Celestial Arts, 1978.

Saunders, Antoinette, and Bonnie Remsberg. *The Stress-Proof Child.* Signet Books, 1984.

Seamands, David A. *Healing of Memories.* Victor Books, 1985.

Schuller, Robert H. *Believe in the God Who Believes in You.* Thomas Nelson Publishers, 1989.

_____. *Self-Esteem: The New Reformation.* Word Books, 1982.

_____. *Self-Love.* Hawthorn Books, Inc., 1969.

Shedd, Charlie W. *You Are Somebody Special.* McGraw-Hill Company, 1978.

Sheehy, Gail. *Passages.* E. P. Dutton and Company, Inc., 1976.

_____. *Pathfinders.* William Morrow & Company, Inc., 1981.

Siegel, Bernie S. *Love, Medicine, and Miracles.* Harper and Row, 1986.

Silvernail, David L. *Developing Positive Student Self-Concept.* National Education Association, Washington, D. C., 1981.

Simmermacher, Donald. *Self-Image Modification: Building Self-Esteem.* Health Communications, Inc., 1981.

Simon, Sidney. *Caring, Feeling, Touching.* Argus Communications, 1976.

_____. *Getting Unstuck.* Warner Books, 1989.

_____. *I Am Lovable and Capable.* Argus Communications, 1973.

_____. *Meeting Yourself Halfway.* Argus Communications, 1974.

_____. *Negative Criticism.* Argus Communications, 1978.

_____. *Values Clarification: A Handbook of Strategies for Teachers and Students.* Hart, 1972.

_____. *Vulture.* Argus Communications, 1977.

Simonton, O. Carl, Stephanie Matthews-Simonton, and James L. Creighton. *Getting Well Again.* Bantam Book, 1978.

Sinetar, Marsha. *Do What You Love, the Money Will Follow.* Dell Publishing, 1987.

Smalley, Gary, and John Trent. *The Blessing.* Thomas Nelson Publishers, 1986.

Spache, George D. *Good Reading for the Disadvantaged Reader.* (Good section on self-concept.) Garrard Publishing Company, 1975.

Steiner, Claude. *The Original Warm Fuzzy Tale.* Jalmar Press, 1977.

Viorst, Judith. *Necessary Losses.* Simon and Schuster, 1986.

Vissell, Joyce, and Barry Vissell. *Models of Love: The Parent-Child Journey.* Ramira Publishing, 1986.

Waitley, Denis. *The Psychology of Winning.* Berkley Books, 1979.

Whitfield, Charles L. *Healing the Child Within.* Health Communications, Inc., 1987.

Wigginton, Eliot. *Sometimes a Shining Moment: The Foxfire Experience.* Anchor Press/Doubleday, 1985.

Wilkerson, David. *Parents on Trial (Why Kids Go Wrong—or Right).* Hawthorn Books, Inc., 1967.

Yamamoto, Kaoru. *The Child and His Image.* (Self-concept in the early years.) Houghton Mifflin Company, 1972.

Yorgason, Blaine M. *Charlie's Monument.* Publishers Press, 1976.

Young, Leotine. *Life Among the Giants.* (A child's eye view of the grown-up world.) McGraw-Hill, 1965.

Young, Paul T. *Motivation and Emotion.* John Wiley and Sons, Inc., 1961.

Zerafa, Judy. *Go for It!* Workman Publishing, 1986.

Ziglar, Zig. *Raising Positive Kids in a Negative World.* Ballantine Books, 1989.

_____. *See You at the Top.* Pelican Publishing Company, 1977.

Please Hear What I'm Not Saying

Please don't be fooled by me.
Don't be fooled by the face I wear,
For I wear a mask. I wear a thousand masks.
Masks that I'm afraid to take off,
And one of them is me.
Pretending is an art that's second nature with me.
But don't be fooled.
I give you the impression that I'm secure.
That all is sunny and unruffled with me.
Within as well as without.
That confidence is my name and coolness my game
And that I need no one.
But please don't believe me.
Please.
My surface may seem smooth, but my surface is my mask,
My ever-varying and ever-concealing mask.
Beneath lies no smugness, no complacence.
Beneath dwells the real me in confusion, in fear, in aloneness,
But I hide this.
I don't want anybody to know it.
I panic at the thought of my weakness and fear being exposed.
That's why I frantically create a mask to hide behind.
A nonchalant, sophisticated facade, to help me pretend.
To shield me from the glance that knows.
But such a glance is precisely my salvation. My only salvation.
And I know it.
That is if it's followed by acceptance.
It's the only thing that can liberate me from myself.
From my own self-built prison walls.
From the barriers that I so painstakingly erect.
It's the only thing that will assure me of what I can't assure myself,
That I'm really worth something.
But I don't tell you this.
I'm afraid your glance will not be followed by acceptance and love, I'm afraid you'll
    think less of me, that you'll laugh, and
Your laugh will wound me.
I'm afraid that deep down inside I'm not much,
And you will see this and reject me,
So I play my game, my pretending game,
With a facade of assurance without.
So when I'm going through my routine do not be fooled by what I'm saying.
Please listen carefully and try to hear what I'm not saying.
What I'd like to be able to say, but can't.
Who am I, you may wonder. I am someone you know very well,
For I am every man you meet, and every woman you meet.

—Author unknown